1996

TEACHING
FROM THE HEART

The Professional Practices in Adult Education and Human Resource Development Series explores issues and concerns of practitioners who work in the broad range of settings in adult and continuing education and human resource development.

The books are intended to provide information and strategies on how to make practice more effective for professionals and those they serve. They are written from a practical viewpoint and provide a forum for instructors, administrators, policy makers, counselors, trainers, managers, program and organizational developers, instructional designers, and other related professionals.

Editorial correspondence should be sent to the Editor-in-Chief:

Michael W. Galbraith
Florida Atlantic University
Department of Educational Leadership
College of Education
Boca Raton, FL 33431

TEACHING
FROM THE HEART

Jerold W. Apps

KRIEGER PUBLISHING COMPANY
MALABAR, FLORIDA
1996

Original Edition 1996

Printed and Published by
KRIEGER PUBLISHING COMPANY
KRIEGER DRIVE
MALABAR, FLORIDA 32950

FROM A DECLARATION OF PRINCIPLES JOINTLY ADOPTED BY A COMMITTEE OF THE AMERICAN BAR ASSOCIATION AND A COMMITTEE OF PUBLISHERS:
This publication is designed to provide accurate and authoritative information in regard to the subject matter covered. It is sold with the understanding that the publisher is not engaged in rendering legal, accounting, or other professional service. If legal advice or other expert assistance is required, the services of a competent professional person should be sought.

Library of Congress Cataloging-In-Publication Data

Apps, Jerold W., 1934–
    Teaching from the heart / by Jerold W. Apps. — Original ed.
        p.   cm. — (The professional practices in adult education and human resource development series)
    Includes bibliographical references (p. 119)
    ISBN 0-89464-940-X (alk. paper)
    1. Adult learning.   2. Teaching.   3. Affective education.
I. Title.   II. Series.
LC5225.L42A67   1996
374'.1—dc20   95-37271
                                                                              CIP

10 9 8 7 6 5 4 3 2

CONTENTS

PART I

LEARNING FROM THE HEART

PART II

TEACHING FROM THE HEART

PREFACE

With changes and challenges swirling around, and with life ever more competitive and hectic, it is time to reexamine teaching and learning. How can we learn in ways that touch the depths of who we are rather than skip across the surface? As teachers, how can we teach in ways that help individuals get in touch with themselves as whole people?

Teaching from the Heart is written for teachers and for learners. Its purpose is to illustrate learning for the whole person, including attending to spiritual, biological, intellectual, and emotional dimensions. Learners will discover, particularly through the stories and the exercises, the meaning of learning from the heart. Teachers will learn how to develop their own such learning, and then explore ways that they can teach from the heart.

Several recent books illustrate the need for people to explore dimensions of their souls, and to become whole people in a time of societal fragmentation and disintegration. See References and For Further Reading. *Teaching from the Heart* builds on this work by offering specific ideas for teaching and expanded perspectives about learning.

This book is divided into two major sections. Part I, Learning from the Heart, includes five chapters. Chapter 1 explains why a new look at learning is needed. Chapter 2 includes stories and an exercise on whole person learning. In Chapter 3, Waking up to Life, the reader, through stories and exercises, discovers the meaning and importance of being fully alive. Chapter 4 is about cycles and spirals of life with exercises on searching for meaning and expressing creativity. Chapter 5 focuses on relationships, including an exercise on life cycles.

Examining the core of who we are is the subject of Chapter

6. It includes exercises on examining personal beliefs and values, and approaches for getting in touch with our hearts. Part II, Teaching from the Heart, consists of five chapters. Chapter 7 includes paradoxes of teaching from the heart, and a credo for such teaching. Chapter 8 includes personal approaches for learning from the heart that teachers can encourage. These include concentration, relaxation, journal writing, reflection, and reclaiming our own truth. Chapter 9 focuses on group approaches for learning, including drawing, using three-dimension materials, sharing journals, listening to music, sharing outdoor experiences, and traveling on a mythical journey. Chapter 10, Challenges, illustrates problems facing those who teach from the heart.

ACKNOWLEDGMENTS

Many people helped me with this book at every level of its creation and writing. I particularly want to thank Dr. Sue Sadowske and Dr. Judy Adrian for reading several drafts and offering many suggestions for improvement. Dr. Robert Pence, who understands heart in learning better than almost anyone, kept me on track and pointed me toward many valuable references. Dr. Marge Engleman, writer, teacher and student of spirituality, read and made invaluable comments about the work.

People who participated in my workshops on learning and in my graduate course on philosophy of adult education, challenged many of the ideas in this book and pushed me toward sharpening my early thinking on this topic.

Susan Horman, a first grade teacher and my daughter, knows what teaching from the heart means from practicing it for many years. She offered many insightful suggestions. Steven Apps, my son, a photojournalist and writer, read and marked up every draft of the manuscript. "What are you trying to say, Dad?" was his favorite comment. My wife Ruth reads all of my material, and in her quiet way keeps me focused and out of the clouds. To all of these people and many more: thank you.

THE AUTHOR

Jerold W. Apps is a writer and an educational consultant for lifelong learning. He is Professor Emeritus of Adult and Continuing Education and former chairperson of the Department of Continuing and Vocational Education at the University of Wisconsin-Madison. He received his B.S. degree and his M.S. degree in agricultural education and his Ph.D. in adult education from the University of Wisconsin-Madison.

Apps's research has focused on new approaches for adult learning as well as leadership in adult education. He has taught workshops and graduate courses throughout North America. In 1988 he was Distinguished Visiting Professor at the University of Alberta, he was Lansdowne Scholar at the University of Victoria in 1990, and Distinguished Visiting Professor in Adult Education at the University of Alaska Anchorage in 1995.

His books include: *How to Improve Adult Education in Your Church* (1972), *Study Skills for Adults Returning to School* (1978), *Problems in Continuing Education* (1979), *The Adult Learner on Campus* (1981), *Improving Your Writing Skills* (1981), *Improving Practice in Continuing Education* (1985), *Higher Education in a Learning Society* (1988), *Study Skills for Today's College Student* (1990), *Mastering the Teaching of Adults* (1991), and *Leadership for the Emerging Age* (1994).

Apps also studies and writes about upper Midwestern history. His books in this area include: *The Land Still Lives* (1970), *Cabin in the Country* (1973), *Village of Roses* (1973), *Barns of Wisconsin* (1977, 1995), *Mills of Wisconsin and the Midwest* (1980), and *Breweries of Wisconsin* (1992). Currently he is researching and writing a book on the history of Wisconsin one-room country schools.

Some of his awards include: best nonfiction book by a Wisconsin writer (1977); best scholarly book by a Wisconsin writer (1985); Historical Book Award of Merit (1978, 1981, 1993); Research to Practice Award (AAACE, 1982); Outstanding Wisconsin Adult Educator of the Year (1987); Outstanding Literary Achievement Award (1993); and Wisconsin Idea Award (1994).

Apps is past president of the Wisconsin Academy of Sciences, Arts and Letters, and past chairman of the North American Commission of Professors of Adult Education. From 1976–1984 he served as consulting editor for the McGraw-Hill Book Company. Apps and his wife Ruth live in Madison and Wild Rose, Wisconsin, where they enjoy canoeing, gardening, and cross-country skiing.

PROLOGUE

A bank of clouds had been building in the west all afternoon, slowly, not perceptible to most of us as we paddled canoes
down the Missouri River from the Garrison Dam on our way to
Bismarck.

This river trip was part of a 2-week workshop for educational leaders. Out on the river, away from telephones and fax
machines, away from classrooms with walls and teachers with
formal lectures, we paddled from early morning until late afternoon. At day's end, we pulled our canoes on shore, built camp-
fires, pitched tents, and recounted the day's activities and the
day's insights and learning.

On this particular day we hurried a little for the clouds were
now building rapidly. In the distance we could hear the low rum-
ble of thunder rolling across the expanse that is western North
Dakota. Before crawling into our tents, we tightened tent ropes
and zipped tent flaps snugly.

Sometime around midnight the storm struck our little tent
village on the banks of the mighty Missouri. Lightning flashed,
making insides of tents as bright as noon before plunging them
back to the deepest of darkness. Thunder rolled up the river,
tumbling back on itself, becoming ever louder as the storm hit
with full force. Sometimes the thunder claps shook the ground
they were so intense.

None of us knew exactly what to expect, although some of
us had spent many nights in tents and had been in many storms.
Thunderstorms are always mysterious, dangerous, and demanding of respect. In many ways the thunderstorm is a metaphor for
the kind of world we are experiencing. We can hear the thunder
and see the lightning, but each storm is different from what we

have previously experienced. And the storms seem closer together; they appear unrelenting, never stopping. These storms in
our lives, and in the lives of our organizations and institutions,
tear at us, challenge us, humble us, and befuddle us. Just when we
think we have things figured out, they change again, not unlike a
thunderstorm that is at the same time familiar and a mystery.

Our old ways of learning, where we studied the past so we
could face the future, are not sufficient in these challenging times.
Likewise, our current ways of teaching, with their often nar-
rowly defined roles for teachers, will not suffice in this age of
mystery and unexpected events. Paradoxically, by examining old
ideas about learning and early ideas about teachers and teaching,
we can gain many insights.

As teachers and as learners we are searching. Sometimes we
are unsure if we are searching for something we have lost or
something we have never had. As we search, what we see is often
out of focus, in the shadows, or so far in the distance that we cannot make out the shapes. The sounds we hear are whispers.
Something from deep within us tells us that these out-of-focus
shapes and unintelligible sounds are important messages, essential messages for our lives, but we can't quite grasp them.

We are in a time when we must learn how to see what is in
the shadows. We are in a time when we must learn how to hear
the whispers. We are in a time when we must recreate the meaning of teaching and of learning. I call these new approaches teaching and learning from the heart.

Part I

Learning from the Heart

CHAPTER 1

A Fresh Look at Teaching and Learning

The first teacher I ever knew taught from the heart. Her name was Theresa Piechowski, and the school was a one-room country school in rural Wisconsin. I was a shy, frightened 5-year-old starting first grade in a school room filled with older kids. Kindergarten hadn't yet come to our community so this was my first experience with schools and teachers.

Miss Piechowski was a strict disciplinarian with a loving heart. She cared about each of us, and she cared about our families and our small, isolated rural community where the nearest crossroads village was 4 miles away and the closest city of about 20,000 people was 30 miles distant.

Miss Piechowski was the janitor (she started the fire in the stove each morning and swept the floors), school nurse (she dealt with everyday bumps and bruises and gave lots of hugs), community leader (she organized school parties and celebrations of various kinds for the entire community), and first and foremost, the teacher (she was responsible for teaching eight grades the basic subjects of reading, writing, arithmetic, history, art, music, and more).

More than 70 years ago, Conrad Patzer (1924) wrote about teachers like Theresa Piechowski.

> A teacher . . . should have a pleasing personality. She should have an attractive personal appearance but this should not necessarily imply physical attractiveness. [Students] are more impressed by the earnestness and interest clothed in the vestment of love and happiness than by any other quality the teacher may possess. It is the inner life of the teacher which appeals to [students]. It is her soul that speaks to them . . . She influences her pupils more by what she is than by what she knows and teaches. (pp. 389–390)

Certain phrases stand out in Patzer's comments: "It is the *inner life of the teacher which appeals . . . It is her soul that speaks to them . . . She influences her [students] more by what she is than by what she knows and teaches.*" Patzer is talking about teaching from the heart.

Since Patzer penned those words, much has happened in the world of teaching and learning. Many educators have lost the essence of his comments as they moved to more "efficient" approaches for teaching and learning. Many educators these days believe that all learning must be practical. They further assume that all learning is ultimately for economic gain, and that teachers provide facts and direction—and in most instances are the experts who "know" and share their "knowing."

Thus teaching and learning have sometimes become technical endeavors no different from feeding raw material into a machine. The person is the learning machine. What is learned is the product. The teacher is the machine operator and a source of raw materials. Simple and straightforward. Feed in facts and information. Use advanced technology such as computers or video machines so boredom doesn't shut down the learning machine. Provide standardized tests to make sure the facts and information "took" and that's it. Simple enough.

WHY THE NEED FOR A DIFFERENT APPROACH?

Before talking about the details of teaching from the heart, let's first explore why it's important to do so. In our world of continuous and capricious change, many of us (teachers included) feel that something is not right in our lives. We are uneasy and restless. Some of us have much less than we had a decade ago. We may have lost our jobs, divorced, lost a loved one, or experienced a serious illness. Others of us have much, but still want more. The more, too often, means more possessions—visible icons of our "success."

For both those of us who have less and those who have more, happiness sometimes seems out of reach. We wonder if our lives will ever have any meaning and purpose anymore. Constantly we fight the clock, trying to do more in less time, racing about each day, and in the evening falling into bed exhausted. Then we awaken in the dark hours of the night, unable to sleep, with a multitude of thoughts and fears. All around us we can feel that the music is changing, but we don't know the words to the new tune.

We are well aware of the changes going on around us—at least at one level. We see computers, information highways, technological advances, scientific breakthroughs in medicine, and sophisticated communication systems. We feel the pressures of our jobs and the challenges our organizations face. We know how difficult it is to find a job that comes close to paying the same as the job we lost.

We recognize political changes in the world. Larger countries break into smaller countries. Smaller countries combine to form large trading blocks such as the North American Free Trade Agreement (NAFTA), and the World Trade Organization resulting from the General Agreement on Tariffs and Trade (GATT).

Poverty is rising in the United States and in many other parts of the world. Illiteracy is increasing. The gap between rich and poor is ever widening. Ethnic groups in various parts of the world are trying to eliminate each other. Diseases such as AIDS baffle those who try to stop its spread.

Willis Harman (1988) says, "The most serious problems of modern society arise from the *successes* of the industrial society paradigm. The horrors of modern warfare, worldwide environmental spoilation, interference with life-supporting ecological systems, progressive resource depletion, widespread poverty and hunger . . ." (p. 111).

Many people are alienated. What results from alienation? Thomas Naylor and Associates (1994) write, "Those who are alienated attempt to defend themselves by being detached from their families, their work, their government, their basic beliefs, and eventually themselves. Drug abuse, alcoholism, divorce, sexual abuse, teenage suicide, crime, and violence are all rooted in meaninglessness" (p. 9).

Underneath the more obvious happenings that I have described above is a set of beliefs that we may not be aware of, but which guide much of the thinking and activity in this country.

These beliefs come from the industrial age that has been a dominant theme in our society for most of the twentieth century. Fritjof Capra (1983) offers several examples of these industrial age beliefs: "the belief in the scientific method as the only valid approach to knowledge, the view of the universe as a mechanical system composed of elementary building blocks; the view of life in society as a competitive struggle for existence; and the belief in unlimited progress to be achieved through economic and technological goals" (p. 31).

We translate these beliefs into phrases that guide our lives: experts have the answers, the world works like a machine, humans are like machines, do more with less, learn how to compete better, earn more money and be happier. These industrial age beliefs and slogans are not serving us well as the world moves beyond the industrial age.

RETHINKING THE FOUNDATIONS
FOR EDUCATION

As we leave behind the industrial age and enter a new time, our old ways of thinking are often outdated and insufficient. We need new assumptions, new ways of thinking, new ways of incorporating mind, body, and spirit into our everyday lives, especially in our learning and in our teaching.

These are baffling times for all of us, especially for teachers. Many people are talking about learning and teaching these days. And everybody, it seems, has an opinion about how to fix whatever problem they believe exists. They have ideas about how to learn better, learn faster, remember more, and apply that learning to making money and leading a happier, more fulfilled life. Those who teach receive an equal amount of suggestion and admonition—do this and students will learn more, become more efficient, get back to the basics, take charge, be in control, learn about the past, study the future, and so on.

Definitions

Before examining several traditional beliefs about education, we must be clear about our definitions. In this book, I use the word *education* to mean teaching and learning whenever and wherever it occurs. Education is often defined as the accumulation of knowledge and skills as in "I have gone to school for 12 years and I have an education." Some equate education with an approach or process as in "Pay attention and I will educate you."

Not denying these uses the word, but going further, I believe *education* is a series of relationships: learners relating to their own intellectual, emotional, physical, and spiritual selves; teachers relating to learners; learners relating to each other; learners relating to knowledge; and teachers and learners relating to contexts and communities.

Formal education occurs in schools, colleges, workplaces, religious institutions, community organizations, and other places where learning and teaching are organized for groups of people.

Informal education includes all teaching and learning that occurs beyond formal education. It includes self-teaching (self-directed learning) and learning through travel, the media, or work—wherever and whenever we learn. It even includes those times when we may not be aware we are learning. Informal education is often an important dimension of formal education; participants in formal educational activities generally learn well beyond and in ways different from what is intended.

Traditional Educational Perspectives

The following perspectives guide much of the education in the world today.

The primary purpose for learning anything is to find a job, advance on a job, or keep a job—primarily economic reasons. Learning beyond the practical is generally viewed as optional or even frivolous. Reading or writing poetry, studying history for the joy of it, or becoming better acquainted with nature are some examples of learning sometimes viewed as frivolous.

We learn in order to maintain the society as we now know it. Or said another way, people learn in order to reproduce the present society with its beliefs, values, slogans, and practices.

Education, like so much of today's society, can be viewed as a machine and described in technical terms. From this position emerge such statements as "All the products of education must be measurable."

Some educational leaders (see Perlman, 1992) advocate "just in time learning." The assumption is that most if not all learning is job-related. People don't need to bother with anything new until it is needed, such as when job requirements shift or new computer software is introduced.

Education, similar to the emphasis in much of society, must become more efficient. One way to become more efficient is to develop "electronic learners," plugged into the information highway as a never ending source of information, stimulation, and alas, too often, manipulation.

Emerging Societal Beliefs

In response to the problems that individuals, families, communities, and much of the world face, an increasing number of people subscribe to beliefs different from those that have been the mainstays of the industrial age: winning at all cost, accumulating possessions, seeing the environment as a consumable resource, depending on specialists, and so on. What are some of these emerging beliefs? (Several of these are drawn from Harman, 1988, pp. 122–125).

Be in harmony with nature. Rather than attempting to conquer nature and use it as a resource, accept that nature and humans are one. Work toward developing interrelationships between people and the natural environment. This is similar to beliefs that Native Americans have long held about the sacredness of the earth and the need to care for it.

Be in harmony with other people. As human beings we are all connected and must rediscover how to relate to each other at many levels. We must rediscover the meaning of community. This implies new forms of relationships between men and women, among ethnic groups, and between those who have long dominated and those who have been subservient. At the same time that individuals are learning to cooperate with each other, they will also learn to respect, accept, and applaud diversity of culture, multiple belief systems, and widely different religious practices. (This is not to suggest that values such as degrading certain humans so others can thrive or mutilating the environment for the sake of economic growth will be tolerated.)

Rediscover the whole person. Realize that humans are complex beings who have many dimensions: intellectual, emotional, physical, and spiritual, all interacting with each other to make the person complete. Accept that the human as learner will involve all of these dimensions, not merely the intellectual.

Redefine knowledge and the ways people relate to it. Accept multiple sources of knowledge—scientific investigation, rational thought, intuition, experts, and the knowledge that people themselves create by living their lives and reflecting on their experiences. Too often we look at knowledge as out there, and it is our task to find it, accumulate it, and put it to some practical use. A new value is one of exploring our interrelationships with knowledge. Parker Palmer (1993) talks about these relationships this way: "We want to teach about Third World cultures in a way that allows us to look at those cultures without ever allowing them to look back at us and to challenge our way of life. We want to teach about the natural world in a way that allows us to analyze it without ever allowing it to criticize our consumptive way of living. We want to teach works of literature in a way that allows us to look at them without allowing those works to examine our own values" (p. 7).

Move beyond seeing everything as "either-or" to a more encompassing view. Include the best of the past in confronting present day problems and challenges. Too often these days, views are narrow and placed in competition with each other: Republicans versus Democrats, labor versus management, personal life versus work life, liberals versus conservatives, religion A versus religion B, and so on. A fresher way is to embrace the diversity of perspectives, including the context and history of the various positions, rather than pitting elements against each other with such statements as "I'm better than you are," or "I'm going to win and you're going to lose."

As we enter a new time, our old assumptions, metaphors, and ways of thinking become outdated and insufficient. We need new assumptions, fresh metaphors, innovative ways of thinking, and novel ways of incorporating mind, body, and spirit into our everyday lives, especially in our learning.

REDEFINING LEARNING AND TEACHING

When I first began teaching adults, the process seemed quite logical. First, figure out what to teach. This usually meant asking people what they wanted to learn, what problems they had, what they were interested in—that sort of thing. Second, write learning objectives. Objectives fell into three categories: change in attitude, change in knowledge, and change in behavior. The last kind was most important; we called these behavioral objectives.

Later, scholars who thought long and hard about objectives and how to write them, said write objectives that could be measured. A cause and effect situation. Teach "X" and expect so many units of "Y."

I was working with rural people, mostly farmers and their families. Typical behavioral objectives were:

• Farmers in X county to increase their corn production by 15%.
• Farmers to experience a 10% decrease in farm equipment maintenance costs

So what were we teaching? We taught how to use high yielding hybrid corn varieties, sufficient amounts of fertilizer, and appropriate weed and insect killers. We taught how to borrow money to purchase more up-to-date machines—whatever it took to increase corn production by at least 15%. Of course the weather could foul up a corn production objective, and it often did, but that is another story.

All of this seemed straightforward, practical, and a way for farmers, in the case of the two objectives cited, to have a few more dollars in their pockets at the end of the growing season. It was hard to argue with this approach, at least I thought so at the time. But what were farmers learning, beyond such technical matters as fertilizer rates, corn varieties, and so on?

They were learning that expert knowledge could help them better their economic situation. They learned that listening to an extension agent (my title) was a way to have a direct hookup to nationally prominent researchers located at the university. They learned that following a recipe (with some modification for different soil types and geographic locations) could result in positive outcomes and that borrowing money was necessary to make money. All this seemed positive enough, but the farmers were learning other things, too, sometimes without being aware of what they were learning.

Many learned to become dependent on outside sources of knowledge—expert knowledge from the university—and quit listening to their internal voices that sometimes offered contradictory perspectives. For instance, many farmers living on sandy soils wondered if heavy applications of nitrogen fertilizer would seep into the groundwater, along with weed killer and insecticide residues (they did). Older farmers remembered that economic cycles occurred on the farm as well as in every other economic enterprise. With economic cycles, it was prudent to keep an eye on land values and farm prices in relation to money borrowed.

Farmers in our classes and workshops learned about short-term results with little attention to long-term consequences. They learned to expect a cause and effect relationship from what they were learning. An increase in the fertilizer applied should result in greater corn yields. They learned to expect that the most important if not the only reason for learning was for economic gain.

And, unfortunately, many of these farmers learned later that going heavily into debt when both land values and farm prices were falling could lead to disaster. Many farmers lost their farms—farms that had been in the same family for generations—because they listened to the advice of experts when their own internal voices might have offered a different perspective. Of course, many other factors contributed to farmers' economic problems.

As thousands of farmers began leaving the land, the extension agents were frustrated. What could they do to help a failed farmer—as they were often called? There was lots of denial on the part of agricultural educators. Many perspectives were offered. The less efficient farmers would eventually have to leave the farm anyway. There were too many farmers and this was one way to even out the numbers.

Some educators tried to help these farmers make a reasonable transition to other work and another kind of life. Much of their educational programming leaned toward counseling rather than offering expert advice on what to do and how to do it. Farmers in crisis didn't want technical knowledge as much as they wanted to consider deeper matters—leaving the land after a lifetime there, losing a farm that their parents and grandparents had owned before them, dealing with their feelings of inadequacy and failure, handling relationships with spouses and children during a period of high stress. These were educational matters more related to the heart than to the head. Extension agents had difficulty with this switch in educational approaches, because now the idea of measurable learning objectives didn't make any sense at all. How silly to write: Twenty percent of displaced farmers to become more comfortable with their circumstances.

The questions these adult educators faced were basic ones. How do you leave behind ideas about teaching and learning built on assumptions about the place for expert knowledge, the role of the teacher, and the mostly economic outcomes? By what means do you change your thinking about what teaching and learning are all about? What can be a foundation for this thinking?

A DIFFERENT PERSPECTIVE

Learning from the heart is a fresh way to think about education. It both builds on traditional approaches to education and challenges them.

Learning from the Heart

Learning from the heart goes beneath the surface. The surface aspects are the accumulation of information, the development of skills, and a change in behavior. Learning from the heart includes surface learning, but also encompasses the exploration of the relationships among the intellectual, emotional, physical, and spiritual dimensions of a person's life, and the relationships of the individual to the community, to the environment, and so on. At an even deeper level, learning from the heart includes discovering what it is to be human and exploring the relationship of *doing* to *being*. Many of us are so busy "doing" that we have forgotten how to "be." We are humans *doing* rather than *human beings*.

Learning requires space. We need intellectual space—an opportunity to try on new ideas, to create new connections. We need spiritual space—a chance to explore the dimensions of our hearts and our relationships, an opportunity to see inside our souls. We need physical space—an occasion for being alone, away from others to stretch our arms and not feel we are invading someone else's place. And, we need emotional space—the opportunity to recognize our feelings and express them.

Everyone is a learner *and* everyone is a teacher. Some people are designated teachers. It is their profession; they are trained to do it. But this doesn't mean that others can't or shouldn't teach. I am not talking about replacing professional teachers, but widening the definition of *teacher*. For instance, when we share our knowledge and experience, and our hopes and fears, we teach. When we ask questions of others, we teach. When we listen to the problems and concerns of people and do nothing more than try to hear, we teach. Within formal educational programs led by professional teachers, everyone can share in the teaching, just as everyone, including the professional teacher, shares in the learning.

The learning focus is on the individual and on the community or collective. Much traditional education has focused solely on the development of the individual. A broader educational perspective includes the individual *and* the community, the individual *and* a relationship to the environment, and so on. Here, teaching and learning is at the same time *inward* and *outward*: toward the person and beyond the person.

Learning includes awe, playfulness, wonder, and mystery. It is not solely a technical activity that always can be planned, predicted, and controlled.

Learning is more than a reaction to stress and crisis, although crisis may open the door to learning. Rather than only a reaction to something, learning is a positive engagement with self, community, and life.

Learning from the heart can provide an underpinning for all learning, from the most technical such as using a new computer software, or performing some new task on a shop floor, to the abstract such as exploring personal relationships or coalescing environmental philosophies. Learning, no matter what its intent, benefits from a connection with the heart.

Learning proceeds in fits and starts. Sometimes it moves forward rapidly with great insights. Often it stalls and learners believe nothing is happening and become frustrated. Sometimes learning slips backward, as people struggle with unlearning something. For many, learning is a spiral, where important themes are visited again and again throughout life, each time at a deeper, more penetrating level.

Learning is often joyous, but sometimes painful and wrenching.

Learning and teaching are courageous acts. They take people into unknown places with unknown outcomes. Sometimes both teachers and learners find themselves in places they do not want to be, and then they seek alternative routes. Few mistakes occur in learning, only surprises that result from risks taken.

Learning takes time. This is particularly so for matters of the heart. It takes a long time to become a human being.

Learning requires a readiness to learn certain things. To encourage people to learn when they are not ready is to invite unpleasantness for all concerned. Not everyone is ready to confront the deeper dimensions of life. Those wrestling with new job skills may not be interested in exploring life's mysteries.

Teaching from the Heart

Teaching from the heart comes from the depths of the teacher as a person. It is not only what the teacher knows, but *who the person is* that makes a difference. Teaching from the heart is an authentic endeavor. The teacher constantly asks, Is what I am doing truly an expression of who I am? And if it is not, why is it not?

Teachers strive to touch the hearts of learners, to form a connection.

The teacher encourages people to take responsibility for their own learning.

Teaching from the heart, rather than replacing well-known teaching approaches, adds to them. It builds on them and takes them deeper. It provides another perspective, an opportunity to work beneath the surface of the obvious to help people get in touch with additional components of their lives.

CHAPTER 2

Whole Person Learning

To teach from the heart, we must know how to learn from the heart. Such learning can occur anywhere and at any time in our lives. It can occur as a part of planned educational programs, but it occurs even more often in unexpected places and at unexpected times.

AN EXAMPLE: FLOYD JEFFERS

Floyd Jeffers came over to see me nearly every day when I was working alone at the shack. When my wife was with me he didn't come, something about interfering I suspected. Floyd had been a tall, thin man when he was younger. Now, in his 70s, he was bent over from a back injury and supported himself with a gnarled, homemade wooden cane that he carried with him everywhere. He walked with a kind of shuffle step that seemed painful, but he never complained. He spoke slowly and deliberately, measuring each word against some standard of worth, or perhaps speaking little in order to conserve his sparse energy.

The shack, as we called the old farm granary, was slowly becoming a livable cabin after many hours of work and endless problems in its restoration. One particularly hot July day, when I was sawing holes in the walls for windows, I saw Floyd shuffling across the road from the farmhouse where he lived alone. I knew he was on his way to see me, and I looked forward to the interruption. Hot days like these were meant for slowing down and taking long brakes, whether enjoying a cold drink or relaxing under a nearby tree.

Having no refrigerator I couldn't offer Floyd an iced drink, but the abandoned well on the place, now back in service, provided cold water to quench the thirst from hot steamy summer days.

"How are you doing, Jerry?" He waved his old cane by way of greeting.

"It's hot," I said, reporting what both of us already knew. Floyd fished out a large red handkerchief and swabbed it across his deeply wrinkled forehead.

Together we sat on a pair of folding chairs, under the shade of hundred year old willow trees strung across the west side of my farmyard.

"Been thinking," Floyd said slowly. He said nothing for a time. I wondered what he was thinking, and eventually wondered if he remembered.

"This old granary," he began again. "Well, I didn't think you'd ever be able to turn it into anything livable. I didn't say that to you before, but that's what I was thinking."

"I figured you thought that way," I answered. I knew that Floyd was a practical man, having been a farmer all his life.

"It's coming along smartly," he said as a grin spread across his face. "I've got a few ideas that might help things along."

And so on that day and several days afterwards, Floyd and I sat in the shade of the black willow trees for an hour or so each day, and he shared his experiences of working with old buildings. It became my daily building seminar, a practical, not-written-anywhere series of suggestions for converting a turn-of-the-century farm granary into a country cabin. The advice included how to remove the smell of horse manure from the building—its most recent use before we naively declared the place a cabin and set out to make it so. And how to remove the accumulation of chicken manure from the walls and even the ceiling of the lean-to building attached to the granary that we had declared a porch. (Lime destroys horse manure smells; liquid disinfectant sweetens the smell of a former chicken coop.)

The seminars were not just general comments about how to rescue old buildings from their natural demise, but specific comments on how to deal with some problem I was facing that day. Clearly, on those hot days in July, Floyd was teacher and I was student as I tried to remember what he was saying (occasionally even writing a note when he mentioned a product that would solve some problem I had).

I looked forward to his daily visits, as much to him and his stories that he wove around his advice as to the advice itself. Together we laughed and talked well beyond the subject of the impromptu seminars—how to restore this derelict old granary. I learned about Floyd's love for the out-of-doors, particularly for deer and songbirds. He kept his bird feeder filled year-round, and he made sure that his farm displayed new "No Trespassing" signs each year before deer hunting season.

We discussed world politics and local problems. We talked about the economy and the dry, hot weather we were having. I learned that Floyd, with but seven or eight years of formal education, was a voracious reader of books, magazines, and newspapers and was thus a font of information on almost any contemporary topic. Besides, of course, he shared the wisdom of his years of living in the country and facing all varieties of problems.

One warm afternoon I noticed that Floyd was carrying something with both hands, his cane stuffed under one arm. Without the cane he moved even more slowly. I was curious. As he came closer, I noticed that he toted a bucket with no handle, filled with what looked like flowers or grass.

Up close I could see that Floyd's bucket was filled with various kinds of wildflowers that were in bloom this time of the year.

"I was wondering," Floyd began as he sat on the chair where he usually sat under the black willow. "I was wondering," he started again, "if you could help me figure out the names of these wildflowers."

That afternoon I became the seminar leader. Floyd jotted down the names of wildflowers as I shared them. For those I didn't know, we thumbed through my wildflower book until we both agreed that what he was holding in his hand was what was pictured in the book.

Looking back at that summer of cabin construction, I now realize that it was also a summer of learning. I was learning much on my own as I tried to develop elementary carpentry skills. But the learning I savored most were the times when Floyd Jeffers shuffled across the road, sat under my old black willow trees, and we talked. At times, as I reflect on it now, Floyd was clearly the teacher and I the learner. At other times, I was teacher and Floyd was learner. And yet, at other times, such as when we together tried to key out a wildflower, we were co-learners.

There was great joy in this learning. It was learning that touched both of us profoundly, although Floyd was not someone who would talk about such things. Neither of us talked about the learning that was going on, and who was teaching. It didn't matter. We had elevated learning and the joy of it well beyond the narrow definitions associated with schooling and professional education.

As two people learning together and learning from each other, we not only were gaining information and developing new skills, but we were sharing ourselves with each other. There were no barriers. It didn't matter on those hot July days that I had a Ph.D. degree and Floyd had not finished elementary school. The topic never came up. There was no concern that in our discussions personal matters might become tangled up with matters so practical as how to remove the smell of horse manure from the premises. Some days we talked for a half hour, other days it was two hours. Somehow we both knew when the discussion was finished for the day and it was time to return to our previous tasks.

That winter, while our partially completed cabin lay buried in snow, we got word that Floyd had died. I grieved the loss of my newly found co-learner. Succeeding summers, although full and exciting, never again included the seminars under the black willow trees, when the hot July sun beat down without mercy. A special kind of learning had taken place that summer. Floyd and I were clearly learning with our hearts as well as with our minds.

What were dimensions of this learning?

- We were both teachers, and we were both learners.
- Credentials and certificates didn't matter in our teaching and our learning.
- What went on was authentic. Neither of us was trying to impress the other. We cared about each other, and we cared about what we were learning and what we were teaching.

- We clearly didn't need a classroom for what we were doing, although classrooms are certainly helpful at times. At least once we had to adjourn to the cabin when a quick rainstorm blew up from the west. The cabin porch became a classroom.
- What we shared came from who we were and what we had experienced. There was no distinction made as to whose experiences were more important.
- No topic was out-of-bounds in our discussions. It all fit.
- No particular teaching approaches were used or even thought about. Our sharing was natural and appropriate for the topic. If we talked about wildflowers, for instance, we looked at, smelled, felt, and got acquainted with wildflowers.
- Stores were often a part of our sharing—stories that triggered the details of our memories and included humor, suspense, and drama.

Some dimensions of that summer seminar went beyond words, well into the realm of the emotional and the spiritual. Learning from the heart is like that.

BEYOND THE CURRICULUM

Learning from the heart can occur in more formal educational situations as well. A few months ago I participated in an awards ceremony at an educational conference in New Jersey. Honorees included the outstanding teacher of the year, people who had created the most innovative programs, the volunteer who contributed the most, and others.

The procedure is generally this. The citation is read, the person comes forward, receives a plaque, says some words of thanks, a few cameras flash, and the person sits.

This time something different happened. The award was for the adult student of the year, someone who had been away from school and then returned. The presenter read the citation: "Here is a unique young woman. She is 32 years old and has a 15-year-old daughter. She has been on drugs, has been arrested several times, and is now in recovery. And she'll receive her diploma at the end of this semester." He then mentioned her name. She slowly walked to the podium to receive her award.

She turned to the microphone, glanced at her newly won walnut plaque, and then looked out over the nearly 500 people assembled in the hall. For a long time she looked at the sea of faces, and said nothing.

"I always wanted to be somebody," she finally said with a loud and clear voice. The room was utter silence. People eating their desserts stopped eating. Recently filled coffee cups remained in their saucers.

"I am ready to graduate and now I feel like I am somebody," she continued. "I am somebody of value."

"This is the first award I've ever gotten," she said. Not a dry eye in the room.

"I have a trophy at home. I stole it. This is the first award that I've ever earned through my own efforts. And it feels good." A thin smile spread across her face. As she returned to her seat, everyone stood and applauded.

She wasn't talking only about the courses she had taken, the skills she had developed, and the knowledge she had gained. She wasn't talking solely about the award she had just received. She was talking about something larger and deeper. She was talking about self-respect and self-worth. She was talking about a beginning that was emerging from the old self she wasn't happy about.

Here, in New Jersey, in a room crowded with educators, I also saw learning from the heart, learning that had a deeper meaning than the accumulation of information and the learning of skills.

What made this experience one of learning from the heart? This young woman was learning about herself. She was discovering dimensions of her life that she wanted to change, and she was proud of what she had accomplished. She was developing self-confidence as she was uncovering a new sense of who she was. She had clearly been confronting some of her personal problems as she studied the prescribed courses in her academic program. The academic work had contributed to her being honored that day in New Jersey. But there was much more. In this instance, what seemed to be the most important learning for this young woman had occurred outside the prescribed curriculum and beyond the day-to-day teaching. Yet, it had occurred at the same time. Learning from the heart is not beyond or separate from traditional learning. It can be integral to it.

Too often as learners, we fail to realize the potential which lies beyond the goals for the course or class or workshop. We enroll to gain new knowledge, develop a skill, or perhaps earn a degree, diploma, or a certificate. These are good reasons for learning. But we fail to realize that learning can be so much more, if we allow it and if the environment encourages it to happen.

Because we have been so conditioned to believe that learning must be identified with formal education, we often overlook the rich opportunities for learning in day-to-day living. All of us have a Floyd Jeffers in our lives, perhaps several of them. A first step in learning from the heart is accepting that talking with someone else, sharing ideas, and attempting to answer each other's questions are powerful ways of learning. The barriers of grades and competition are missing.

We can also learn from situations that life throws in our path. We can learn when we face some unexpected event, something as simple as a leaky faucet or a car that won't start on a cold morning, or something as devastating as the death of a loved one or the loss of a job.

As a person responsible for our own learning, we can take much of our learning deeper. We can, through our own efforts, allow our learning to flow well beyond the intentions of the educational program we are enrolled in or the life situation in which we are immersed.

Beyond formal education, where much of the learning is preset by course requirements, and beyond, too, learning associated with life events, we can design our own learning projects for probing into the mysteries of life and living. Through our own learning programs, we can challenge ourselves to relate what we are learning to who we are becoming.

BECOMING MORE HUMAN

Too often these days, learning is viewed as a means toward a better job, an increase in salary, or a requirement for keeping one's job. In some instances we are forced to attend a course or workshop because we violated some law. Learning is part of our punishment.

For many young people attending elementary and secondary schools, learning is something to do while waiting to do something else. By the time that many of them reach the age where they no longer are required to attend school, they drop out. These young people are soured on learning and see only its negatives.

Many of us have never realized that learning can make us human, can help us get up each day with anticipation and excitement, and can help us to live our days with meaning rather than with remorse, guilt, and a host of other demons that drag us down and make us less than what we could be.

Unfortunately, we have not known real learning because we have spent a lifetime learning what others have told us to learn or even sometimes forced us to learn. Learning has been anything but joyful.

Many of us learn to earn. There is often little joy in this learning, particularly when the learning is organized so that we must learn in lockstep with our peers, and our learning is constantly compared with our fellow learners—in the name of "achieving excellence."

I do not deny the importance of work-related learning, only the way that is usually offered. There is little heart in learning that is mechanical and machine-like, where the learner is treated like a machine that needs a tune-up. We even use machine language: "Susan has rusty office skills," or "Joe needs a bit of re-tooling." Rub off the rust, smear on a new coat of paint, and the machine will operate like new, maybe even better. Add some new parts and perhaps remove some old ones and the machine will be able to do a new job.

Educational technology such as interactive computers, E-mail systems, satellite communication, and the like will change the nature of education and, for some, provide new and expanded opportunities to learn. But this kind of learning is often more of the old kind of learning in newly wrapped technological packages. The focus of such educational communications is on helping people develop skills and get information for the purpose of making them more productive workers.

As we become more comfortable with technology-assisted learning, with increasing dependence on machines to help us, how do we avoid allowing the machine to dictate not only *what* we think but *how* we think? How do we learn from the heart in an environment that assumes that the major reason for learning is to become an ever more productive citizen? Becoming a productive citizen is certainly an important reason for learning, but it falls far short of the vast potential that learning can provide. Where within a technological approach to learning can we work toward becoming more human? Where in such a highly technical approach to learning can we wrestle with the challenges of life that are not related directly to our productivity, such as discovering the meaning of relationships between the community, the environment, and ourselves?

WHOLE PERSON LEARNING

Most of us believe we learn only with our heads. We don't realize that we are a connected wholeness—a combination of intellect, emotion, spirit, and body.

To learn as a whole person, we must listen for the whispers from our hearts and the messages from our bodies. Of course we involve our minds, but we avoid concluding that thought and thinking are the beginning and end of learning.

We have become people of the mind and have forgotten how to also become people of the heart. When I was a youngster, growing up on a Central Wisconsin farm, much of my learning was whole person learning. I didn't call it that. I didn't even call it learning for I was brought up believing that important learning occurred only in schools.

One spring, when I was in high school, a windstorm swirled through out neighborhood, toppling a portion of our cattle barn and partially burying my favorite calf. My father had given me this calf as payment for my summer work on the farm. When I hurried out to the barn that early, eerie morning in May to find my calf buried in rubble, I burst into tears.

Frantically I dug away the rubble and discovered the animal was still breathing. It had a broken leg and likely a broken back as well. A neighbor told me to destroy it, that a crippled calf was worthless around a farm. He volunteered to do the job for me, but I wouldn't let him.

That spring I nursed my calf back to health. My father showed me how to splint the broken front leg. I quickly learned what the calf would eat and what it would not. I discovered how to lift the calf to its feet and taught it to walk again. By midsummer my calf was walking, running, and growing like the other calves.

Reflecting back on that experience, my head told me the neighbor was right. A severely injured animal should be destroyed. But a voice inside of me said to give healing a chance. And I did. And the voice was right.

I learned many skills that spring about caring for an injured animal. But more importantly, I learned about caring, about patience, about hope and fear, and about the shadow of death that hung over my calf for several days after we had removed it from the rubble.

Whole person learning means listening to what our mind says, but also listening to that quiet voice that comes from the heart and is filled with a perspective that helps make learning whole.

EXERCISE 2.1 LEARNING AS A WHOLE PERSON

Recall an event or a time when you learned as a whole person, where your intellect, emotions, body, and spirit were all involved.

- What were you learning?
- What were the circumstances?
- Besides yourself, who was involved?
- What happened?
- What feelings do you recall about the event?
- What can you learn by reflecting on that event today?

LEARNING DEEPLY

When we involve all of ourselves, we can learn more deeply. Sometimes we don't know what we have learned in a situation until we come back to it in our minds and reflect on it. To learn deeply about something, we sometimes need distance. We need some perspective.

Each year I canoe in the Boundary Waters of northern Minnesota, where no motors are allowed and the number of visitors is limited. There is meaning that comes from the moment—insights, new understandings, new information accumulated, even some unexpected learning as I face a new situation and must learn to make the most of it while I am in the middle of it. For instance, one early morning, with our canoe fully loaded after leaving our camp for a new site, my son and I paddled slowly across a small, glass-smooth lake toward the portage. The sun was slowly lifting above the trees and beginning to burn off the morning mists that hung over the lake, creating strange images and sometimes playing tricks on the eyes.

I noticed what appeared to be a rock in the water and pointed my paddle at it so my son would see. But the rock began moving and growing larger. A cow moose, nearly submerged, came into focus. When she saw us, she began moving toward shore and would cross our path. We slowed the canoe and watched, hoping that the moose would continue toward shore and not decide that we were a threat to her calf which was likely waiting in the underbrush.

We sat motionlessly, doing nothing to alarm this huge beast. She was in her home environment while we were clearly not. As the moose edged closer to shore and began emerging from the water, she appeared larger and larger. In the mists she seemed even larger than she was. Once out of the water, she shook herself as a big dog might, glanced toward us, and disappeared into the woods.

Our decision to slow and remain motionless was the right one. In the midst of sleepily paddling across this quite lake, an immediate decision was necessary. In our many years of canoeing, we had never come on a moose in mid-lake, so we had no prior learning on which to draw. Experience, however, had taught us that in some situations the best action is no action, and that is what we decided to do. We were trying to make the most of the situation while we were in the midst of it. Had she chosen to take us on, we likely would have made quite a different decision.

Learning at a deeper level requires some distancing and some work. Learning from the heart takes time and often requires solitude.

As I think about the moose in the quiet lake on a misty morning, and my son and I in a fully loaded canoe, I reflect on what I learned from that situation. At the time, we were elated that the moose didn't come at us for she could probably swim faster than we could paddle. Now, as I reflect on the situation, I remember the beauty of the lake in the morning, the majesty of this cow moose, and the possible danger we might have faced. I believe our action of taking no action was appropriate for the situation. But the learning from that situation goes well beyond tucking away how to behave when facing a moose in its territory. At another level, the experience, one of many I have had since I was a child, connected me with the natural environment and helped to realize that when I am in the out-of-doors I often face entirely new experiences. Not only do these new experiences often test my mettle, but they keep me united with something that is much larger than I am as a person. I regularly need these connections, I long ago decided. And I need to experience them firsthand whenever I can. Reading a book about how someone faced down a moose on a misty morning is not good enough.

Learning more deeply takes practice and discipline. We must push ourselves to see things more profoundly, to feel more intensely, and to allow our minds to explore experiences more broadly. For many persons this is not easy. The inner censor that each of us has asks, why bother examining old experiences when there are new things to learn? Such learning can evoke fright as well as elation. Deep-seated beliefs and values are challenged. Long-held ideas are found wanting.

Yet, learning from the heart combines the physical, the intellectual, the emotional, and the spiritual dimensions of our being in such a way that we begin to touch the essence of our humanity. We begin to touch our souls.

CHAPTER 3

Waking up to Life

For years I rushed here and there—taught my classes, con-
ducted research, flew off somewhere to lecture and conduct
workshops, spent little time with my wife and children, and contributed little to my community.

I lived my life in the future. I worried about tomorrow's
meeting, my next speech, the upcoming workshop, and the re-
port due in two weeks. When I wasn't worrying about some future responsibility, I worried about something that had gone
wrong in the past. I forgot how to live in the moment, to focus
on and appreciate what was happening right now. I carried my
appointment calendar with me everywhere and without realizing
it let my calendar control me.

One cold winter day I had an experience at my farm in Central Wisconsin that began to change me. I was hiking through the
snow, down the hill from my cabin and alongside the frozen
pond in the valley. A brisk northwest wind chased little snow
patterns across the pond's once glassy surface. The snow designs
were ever changing as the wind swirled, a kaleidoscope of undu-
lating white.

The wind sighed softly through the tops of the naked
maples, aspen, and birch that surrounded the pond. For a long
time I stood motionless, feeling like an intruder in this land of
white and every changing snow images. The longer I stood listening and watching, feeling the wind on my skin, the more I began to sense a oneness. Although difficult to describe, the experience was at the same time one of calmness and excitement, of
seeing specifics and feeling something much larger. I saw, felt,
heard, and touched the details of what was happening, and at the
same time experienced something that went well beyond what

my senses could comprehend. Though the temperature was bone-chilling, I wasn't cold. The cold seemed to add to the depth of the experience. For me, this was clearly a spiritual encounter, a time when the wholeness of who I am was touched, and shaken a bit.

REDISCOVERING ALIVENESS

Learning from the heart is waking up to life and discovering what it means to live. In our haste and hurry, and in our zeal to compete and accumulate, we often don't take time to experience the joy of being alive.

Being alive means experiencing the moment, whether standing by a windswept snowy pond, talking with a friend, or striving to complete a project at work. Barbara DeAngelis (1994) calls these "real moments." She says, "Real moments occur only when you are consciously and completely experiencing where you are, what you are doing, and how you are feeling . . . you are paying attention, so you will notice things you wouldn't normally perceive if you were not paying attention. There is nothing else in your awareness but the experience you are having" (p. 25).

EXERCISE 3.1   FEELING FULLY ALIVE

- Recall a time when you felt fully alive.
- Describe the situation. What were the details?
- What were you doing?
- What were you feeling?
- How do you feel about that situation today?
- As you reflect on that situation, what do you believe you learned from it?

Many factors prevent us from feeling fully alive—our stress-filled jobs where employers expect always more and our hectic family lives with family members scattered to the winds each day, gathering for a few hours each night, but scarcely having time to speak to each other.

EXERCISE 3.2   BARRIERS TO FEELING
FULLY ALIVE

- List 10 to 12 things that prevent you from feeling fully alive.
- Put them in order with the greatest barriers first.
- Through the process of developing the list, did you discover some barriers that you hadn't previously considered? What were they?
- Which barriers do you want to remove? Chapter 8 includes strategies for overcoming barriers.

BARRIERS TO FEELING FULLY ALIVE

The following are barriers that prevent people from feeling fully alive.

Never Experienced It

Lamentable, but true. Many have never known what it is to be fully alive. Some have been disillusioned into believing that a high obtained from drugs or alcohol is being fully alive. For others, each day is tediously similar to the previous day and the day to come. For an assortment of reasons, they have resolved themselves to expecting little from life, and that is what they experience.

When I was a youngster, when we came to a pond we skipped rocks across the water. A well-thrown rock would skip four or five times or more, briefly touching the water and then rising and touching the water again. Many of us live our lives like that rock. We dip into life from time to time, but we never really experience it. We don't take the time to swim in the water. Unfortunately, by skipping across the surface we may never know what immersion means. We come to accept life as a series of brief encounters before we move on to the next experience.

Others who have never experienced being fully alive expect much from life, but the expectations are external—the accumulation of external goods or the collection of awards, promotions, and other visible achievements. When they stop for a moment to look at their collections, we often hear the cliche, Is this all there is? They have not experienced being fully alive, and they wonder if there is an alternative to collecting.

Fear

A fear of commitment to ourselves, and a fear of what we will uncover prevent many of us from waking up to life. Using the metaphor of the river helps me to appreciate the terror that can overcome people as they attempt to live more fully. A river flows ever onward, never stopping, and never the same. Its sameness is its ever changing nature. We can choose to cling to the riverbank as the river flows by. Or, we can slip a canoe into the river and become one with it. At first, fright grabs us as we move with the strong current and bump into rocks and race through rapids. As we adjust to the river, we learn to relax. Becoming more experienced canoeists, we learn to control many of our movements, which allows us to avoid crashing into rocks. At times, we even paddle upstream, defying the natural direction of the water.

Floating along, we see others still clinging to the banks, fearful of the river and what it will do to them. When we work toward living more fully and learning from the heart, we are like the inexperienced canoeist with the courage to let go of the riverbank not knowing what dangers may lurk around the bend. Inside this courageous canoeist is a feeling that jumping into the river of life and experiencing it, though scary and unpredictable, will be more gratifying and fulfilling than sitting on shore and watching life flow by. Jumping into the river is surely one way to wake up to life.

Life in a Box

An outcome of our highly specialized society is categories (boxes) for everything. Knowledge is well boxed into disciplines such as sociology, psychology, mathematics, physics, and biology. Often we see ourselves as a series of boxes. For instance, to attend to our intellectual self, we attend schools and colleges. For our emotional needs, we visit counselors and therapists. We visit religious institutions for our spiritual needs and periodically a physician checks the condition of our physical health. Seldom do we put it together. We treat ourselves as if we were four different persons: an intellectual person, an emotional person, a spiritual person, and a physical person.

Bring fully alive means seeing ourselves as whole people, attending to each of the dimensions of our being, but also realizing that each dimension of self interacts with every other one. When we are physically ill, our illness affects our intellectual ability, may create emotional havoc, and can cause our spirit to languish. Likewise, emotional problems can cause physical illness. Learning from the heart means learning as a whole person.

Lack of Time

I've heard it often, "I'm too busy making a living to consider what you're talking about." We have become overly busy people, constantly on the go, constantly doing something, and when we are supposed to be relaxing, we continue doing, nonstop. Our lives have become one giant train ride that never ends, on a track that leads to nowhere. Fear prevents us from yelling, "Stop the train, I want to get off." The ride may be rough at times, and the cars crowded with other frantic travelers, but fear of the unknown is a greater fear than remaining on the train.

Becoming fully alive comes from learning from the heart, which takes time, patience, and persistence. As we take time to wake up to life, we sense a feeling of total fulfillment, and we wonder why we didn't step off the train to nowhere a long time ago.

Loss of Wonder and Mystery

Wonder and mystery are for children, we frequently say. Adults must wrestle with matters more serious. To wake up to life, we must continue to cultivate our sense of wonder and childlike innocence of what we confront in life. My little grandson is teaching me how to do this once again. As we walk around the farm and see something he hasn't seen before, his eyes get bigger.

He immediately wants to touch it and taste it and get acquainted with it—whether it is a tree, a wildflower, or a butterfly. He isn't interested in naming what something is, a common tendency as we grow older. But, too often, with the naming we stop. Having a name seems good enough as we discover a new wildflower, for example. We search in our guidebook for the name, and when we find it, we go on to identifying another one. Waking up to life means going beyond the name, getting acquainted beyond the category, attending to all of our senses as we try to get acquainted with what is new in our experience. We can become acquainted at another level with something that is commonplace in our life, but that we've never taken the time to appreciate, enjoy, or really understand. For instance, when was the last time you ate a meal and really took time to taste it, smell it, and enjoy the visual image it created?

As we encounter new experiences, our tendency is to immediately search for a category from our past. If it doesn't fit, we force a fit. If it still doesn't fit, we discard it. This is the dilemma of those who have a multitude of categories into which new encounters are placed. The freshness of new ideas is often destroyed, and the possibility of new ways of thinking is prevented. The possibility of living life more fully is shortchanged.

Internal Turmoil

For many of us, our minds are cluttered with the pressures of everyday life. We worry about our children, our health, our jobs, and the future, about almost everything that comes along. Waking up to life means calming the raging turmoil that engulfs us in those moments when we are away from our incessant doing. Diane Dreher (1990) writes, "Only when we find peace within ourselves can we see more clearly, act more effectively, cooperating with the energies within and around us . . ." (p. xiii)

Excessive Planning

Planning has been accepted by many as the only way toward success and the good life. Visit any stationery store. Many have separate sections for "planners," thick books where we can write our goals and our strategies for achieving them, plus record our appointments, keep records, and so on.

In our jobs we are forever planning. Most of us have sat through long hours of meetings on planning the future for our company, our school, wherever we work. As Sam Keen and Anne Valley-Fox (1989) say, "If we plan too much, we're always living ahead of ourselves, rehearsing scenes that usually don't happen. . . . Those who live in the future miss many of the pleasures of the present" (p. 100).

This does not mean we quit planning. Indeed not. We need a sense of direction. But, on balance, we've got to live less of our lives in tomorrow so that we have time to live today.

EXERCISE 3.3   WAKING UP TO LIFE

As a way to wake up to life and the whole person that you are, try this simple exercise:

Find a place where you can sit quietly, without outside sounds or images interfering.

Breathe deeply. Concentrate on your breathing. As you breath in, say to yourself, in. As you breath out, say to yourself, out.

Allow yourself to be in the moment. Attend only to your breathing for a time, leaving behind your concerns for yesterday and your plans for tomorrow. Now get in touch with your physical self. You may recognize a sore muscle from biking too long, a tension in your neck, a dull ache in your lower back, or some other pain. Concentrate on the pain, allowing yourself to experience it fully. Continue breathing deeply. Experience your physical self completely, beyond your pains and tensions. Concentrate on your physical self, that wonderful biological creation that has served you well for many years.

Once again, focus on your breathing. Reflect on any emotional difficulty troubling you. Anyone with whom you are angry, any loss for which you are grieving. Loneliness, joy, and elation and many other emotions may rise to the surface. Attend to them. Concentrate on them. Feel them fully.

As you continue relaxing and breathing deeply, concentrate on a problem you are trying to solve or a thought that is nagging you.

Do not try to solve the problem or resolve the thought, but concentrate on your power to think and the wonderful gift that it is.

Finally, concentrate on your spiritual nature. Connections are one dimension of our spiritual nature. We connect with other human beings, with communities, with the environment, and for some of us, with an external force. We also seek connections with ourselves.

Concentrate on connecting your physical being with your emotions, and your thoughts. Experience yourself as a whole person, not merely a creature who has physical, emotional, intellectual, and spiritual dimensions. Continue relaxing and allow yourself to go ever deeper inside yourself to discover feelings of wholeness. Then allow yourself to move outside yourself and recognize your connections to everything beyond you.

When you have completed the exercise, reflect on it. Did any surprises emerge? What were they? How do you feel about the exercise now that it is completed? What did you learn from it?

To learn from the heart, and to teach from the heart require that we be fully alive—that we are not only aware of our pasts and concerned for the future, but also able to enjoy and respond to the present. After all, the past is history and the future is a mystery. The present is all we've got.

CHAPTER 4

Cycles and Spirals

A few years ago, my friend Allen Strang phoned me. He said he had something to discuss and he'd buy lunch. Allen had recently retired from the architectural firm he founded and had begun to paint watercolors of old barns, a subject not difficult to find in rural Wisconsin. He wanted to publish a book of his paintings and wondered if I would write the narration.

After a few more meetings, including a session with a publisher, we went ahead with the book. Allen continued painting, and I began writing. From the very beginning I wondered why this 70-year-old architect had decided to do watercolor painting in his retirement. I also wondered how someone who was supposedly just beginning could so quickly develop publishable material. I'd known others who began painting as retirement projects, but none created such fine work as Allen.

One day I asked him why he decided to paint in his retirement. He laughed. "Watercolor painting isn't new with me. When I graduated with a degree in architecture some 40 years ago, I won a scholarship to study watercolor painting in France. All these years I've been so busy when my architectural business I never got back to painting. Now I have time."

So it wasn't a new project, but a return to an earlier project after many years away.

We live our lives in cycles, returning to themes that were important to us at earlier times. Hopefully, most of us don't wait 40 years to do it, as Allen Strang did.

I grew up on a farm and although I moved to the city when I was 16, I have regularly returned to the land year after year. In 1966, I bought a small farm, and as the years have passed, I continue farming a little every year. Part of who I am is tied to the land and the out-of-doors, and I find returning to the soil a rejuvenation of my spirit.

We return to themes in other ways as well. Nearly 30 years ago I became interested in different approaches for teaching adults. I return to that topic regularly, sometimes with new questions, and often in search of new answers to old questions. When people read my early writings about teaching adults, they seem surprised with what I am writing now, particularly when they discover that some of what I say now contradicts what I said earlier. I try to help them understand that I am changing as the years pass, and so is everything else. Thus I am compelled to constantly revisit old questions and old answers, my own and those of others.

I believe that one of the reasons many teachers face "burn out" in their work is because they are not taking time to visit old themes at new levels. Most of us came to teaching filled with excitement and determined to do the best possible job. But for some of us, the months and years pass, and the excitement begins to wane. Occasionally our workload becomes so great and we have so many teaching commitments that there seems no time to raise new questions or attempt to examine old questions in new ways. We become cogs in an ever more demanding machine that requires us to perform day after day. Yet, as Richard Bach (1977) says so well, "You teach best what you most need to learn" (p. 48). And this means pushing out and beyond where we are now.

As we encourage participants in our workshops and classes to explore their own life themes, we must do the same for ourselves. It is difficult to encourage learning from the heart—one dimension of which is to explore life themes in ever greater depth—if we don't take time to do it. We can't give what we don't have.

CYCLING AND SPIRALING

For many of us the ideas of cycling and spiraling are new. Much of our training has been linear, not cyclic. We believe that life is linear. As a result, we regard learning as a linear process. Frederic Hudson (1991) writes, "Linear means 'in a straight line'. . . . According to this point of view, adult life progresses through predictable sequences: learning, loving, working, living, leading, and succeeding. In linear thinking, adult life is viewed as an orderly development following universal principles and rules. Life is lived for future goals and results, and is driven by perfectionism and social constraints" (p. 30).

But we do not learn in straight lines. A person may learn rapidly for a time, moving forward and then stop, plateau, and even slide backward before moving forward again. While one person is moving forward rapidly, another may be slipping backward. Each person has a unique learning journey.

We also do not live our lives in straight lines—born, learn, earn, retire, and die—but in cycles. We regularly return to themes we have previously visited. As Diane Dreher (1990) points out, "We are part of a universal pattern of growth which renews itself in cycles" (p. 5). Our lives are like twisty trails that constantly turn back on themselves, with many beginnings, constant learning, and occasional "death" when we close out a theme in our lives and move on.

LIFE THEMES

Although we may be cycling through life, returning to the same themes from time to time, we have the potential for returning to old themes at new and deeper levels. Some of the themes we confront throughout our lives include the following:

Developing relationships. This includes relationships with our parents, siblings, friends, employers, lovers, communities, the environment, and of course with ourselves.

Searching for meaning. Thomas Naylor and associates (1994) write that many people in our society face a life of meaninglessness as they go about their daily duties, each day identical to the day that preceded it. Naylor says "The price of meaninglessness is nothingness, which is more than most souls can tolerate" (p. 36). To avoid the meaningless in their lives, some people become workaholics on an endless quest to accumulate power, money, and material possessions, or they avoid the reality of their lives through alcohol and drugs. These activities do not lead to meaning in life, but to the avoidance of it. Many of our organizations and institutions reward those who are "never stop workers." People who thirst for meaning and seldom uncover it are found in classrooms, boardrooms, university offices, and about every place where human beings work.

EXERCISE 4.1   SEARCHING FOR MEANING

A beginning place in searching for meaning in one's life is to answer several basic questions:

- What am I doing?
- Why am I doing it?
- Where have I been?
- Where am I going?
- When do I feel most connected?

As Richard Bach (1977) says, "The simplest questions are the most profound . . . think about these once in awhile, and watch your answers change" (p. 47).

Exploring creativity. Within each of us is a creative spirit, sometimes locked tightly away. Sark (1991) says, "We all started out creatively free. Remember the sandbox? All you needed were bare toes on warm sand, and maybe a good bucket. Then you could build your own world" (p. 1). For many of us, our creative spirit has been pushed into the background. In my creative writing classes, I begin by helping people reconnect with their creative spirits. For some this means going back to their childhood, the last time when they believed they really had a chance to express themselves creatively. Yet, I believe that creativity is an integral part of being human. We can express our creativity—through writing, painting, music, or gardening, or through managing, teaching, and relating to people—in hundreds of ways.

EXERCISE 4.2 EXPRESSING CREATIVITY

Do you have an opportunity to regularly express your creativity?

- Recall a recent time when you were being creative.
- What were the circumstances of the situation? Did it happen spontaneously or did you seek to do something creative?
- Describe what you did. What happened?
- Describe the feelings you have now as you recall the event.

Confronting mortality. "The ultimate boundary to human life is death, and for thousands of years we have tried to travel beyond the boundary" (Chopra, 1993, p. 279). When we are young and vibrant, the idea of dying is furthest from our minds. We believe we are invincible and will live forever. Then a loved one dies and we, often for the first time, face the fact of our own mortality. As we age, and experience various health problems, we return to the theme of our mortality. It's a tough theme. We want to avoid it, push it aside, deny it, and make fun of it. But it is always there, and it is a theme worthy of our attention. As we come to understand our dying, we can develop new insights about our living.

Revisiting our personal histories. We all have a history. Many of us try to deny our upbringing, or at least some important part of it. As we live our lives, we return to our histories. We need not let our histories dictate our lives today, but if we are unclear about our histories, how do we know how much of what we are today is a product of our yesterdays?

Knowing ourselves. The oldest of questions remains one of the most contemporary: Who am I? How do I describe myself to myself and to others? How does who I am change as I age? How does who I am change as I relate to others? As someone once wrote, "Without you, I cannot be me."

REVISITING LIFE THEMES

If we take a chance and revisit life themes, we have a great opportunity for learning. Each time we confront a life theme, we learn more deeply. This is true of all the themes, from examining our life histories, to confronting our mortality, to searching for meaning, to developing relationships, to exploring creativity. Mary Catherine Bateson (1994) calls this spiral learning. She writes, "Spiral learning moves through complexity with partial understanding, allowing for later returns. For some people, what is ambiguous and not immediately applicable is discarded, while for others, much that is unclear is vaguely retained, taken in with peripheral vision for possible later clarification, hard to correct unless it is made explicit" (p. 31).

As our life themes present themselves to us again and again over the years, we sometimes ignore the opportunity to explore a theme more deeply. We may believe we do not have the time, or we fear tackling it. We don't know what demons will turn up, so we let the issue rest. Visiting old themes can appear as depressing evidence that we are stuck and haven't grown. When this occurs, a teacher can help reframe the experience, and assist the person to revisit an old theme with new eyes.

As we learn more deeply, we arrive at the humbling reality that there is always more to learn. Thus there is no such thing as mastery, only a moving toward mastery with the full knowledge that we will never know all there is about a given theme. This fact is at the same time the joy and the despair of learning from the heart. Sometimes we ask in desperation, "When will this learning end?" And the answer is "Never," unless we wish constantly to fight deeper learning and resist trying to wrestle with the insights that returning to life themes presents us. We cannot avoid facing them. But we can botch the opportunities for learning, stagnate and try to coast through life, skipping across the surface.

Intended Revisits

Most of us return to certain life themes regularly, and on purpose, by working the visits into our lives. For example, if I can't do something creative, I feel stale and unfulfilled. Writing for me is a creative activity. If I am away from my writing for several days, I have this strong sense of something missing. The same happens when I am away from my farm too long. My wife spots my need before I do. "It's time for you to go to the farm," she will say. I know exactly what she means.

Occasionally we push ourselves toward revisiting a life theme, knowing that the visit can have both painful and joyful results. For many years I've taught life story writing at various writing workshops. In my workshops I offer a series of exercises to help people recall earlier experiences in their lives. Some of the recalled memories are extremely humorous, but others uncover difficult times in the person's life. Often these difficult times concern relationships—a failed marriage, a strained relationship with a parent, or a soured relationship with a sibling.

I recall clearly a man in his 60s, a practicing psychiatrist, who was writing about and wrestling with the relationship with his now dead father. He shared his writings with the workshop group, and it became clear that he had confronted this issue many times in his life. He said the reason he enrolled in the workshop was to return to this theme. The week was a difficult one for him and he certainly didn't resolve the issue of his relationship with his father. But he took the resolution a bit further than he had before.

Unintended Revisits

Sometimes we are forced into revisiting a life theme without intending to do so. We lose our job, we start a new job, we get married, a loved one dies, we become seriously ill, or a long-time personal relationship comes apart.

Alan Jones (1985) calls these "events that stop the world." Jones writes, These world-stopping events are ". . . the means by which we break out, or are broken out of a way of thinking and believing that confuses our descriptions of things, people and events for the realities themselves. This breaking out not only widens our vision, it changes it" (p. 70).

DRAMATIC LIFE CHANGES

As we learn from the heart and confront life themes at ever deeper levels, we sometimes experience a dramatic change in our lives. Some authors such as Jack Meizrow and associates (1990) and Stephen Brookfield (1987) refer to this as a transformation. Other writers, William Bridges (1980) for example, call this dramatic change a life transition. No matter what label is used, to experience a dramatic life change and all that leads up to the change is learning from the heart at the deepest level. Although a life change is often painful and filled with anxiety, tension, and ambiguity, we are never more alive than when we are in the midst of it. Unfortunately, some of us try to avoid change. We prevent ourselves from going deep into ourselves. We try to cover up, forget, deny, and do whatever we can to sidestep accepting change. We hope that we can go back to when we were comfortable (or thought we were) and continue our lives, but once we have experienced one of the "events that stop the world," there is no going back.

In my experience with dramatic life changes, I see a general pattern. Using a metaphor of a knotted rope is a way for me to understand what is happening. The phases in the process include:

Untying the knot
Being at loose ends
Reconnecting

Untying the Knot

In the first phase of a dramatic life change, the rope is untied. For many of us, our lives are well tied together, but then, as Jones (1985) suggests, we experience an event that stops the world. One of our parents dies. We lose our job. Our doctor tells us we have a serious illness. We face a crisis and our rope becomes untied.

We become uncomfortable when part of our life is untied. As the metaphor suggests, we are "at loose ends." We try to tie things together again as quickly as possible. No one wants to be at loose ends for long and besides, we were comfortable with the old knot; it served us well for many years. We even have difficulty accepting why the knot came untied; we usually don't intend for the untying to occur. For instance, we don't anticipate how a loved one's death will affect us. We knew it would happen sooner or later. Then it happens, and it touches us far more profoundly than we ever imagined it would.

We try to retie the knot just as it was, and we discover that we can't do it. There is no turning back. The woman who began writing about sexual abuse couldn't go back. She couldn't hide the memories once she began sharing them. There was no way to retie the knot.

Being at Loose Ends

Clearly, the difficult part of a dramatic life change is when we are at loose ends. Here is when we are most vulnerable, most unsure, and most human. We are in the midst of what Bridges (1980) calls the "neutral zone." "For many people the experience of the neutral zone is essentially one of emptiness in which the old reality looks transparent and nothing feels solid any more" (p. 117).

In the midst of nothingness and emptiness is an opportunity to get in touch with our hearts, for profound learning, for the opportunity to develop new ties. But before we can develop the new ties, before they make sense to us, we must experience our loose ends. We need to allow ourselves the time to explore, to think, to not explore, to avoid thinking. We confront the nothingness of not knowing. We allow ourselves to be patient and to be confident in our uncomfortableness and insecurity. We may experience great sadness and undergo a time of mourning. We grieve the loss of our old connections, old ideas, and old comfortableness. "Our tears prepare the ground for our future growth. Without this creative moistening, we may remain barren. We must allow the bolt of pain to strike us. Remember this is useful pain; lightning illuminates" (Cameron, 1992, p. 7).

Societal expectations run counter to what is needed during this phase of a dramatic change. There is an unspoken societal assumption that we should know where we are going and what

comes next. When we are at loose ends, we just don't know. And
it is in the vacuum of not knowing that the new emerges. It is in
the void of not knowing where to turn or what to do that we are
thrust toward encountering the heart of who we are.

Many people thrust into a dramatic life change seek out
solitude. They go off alone, to a hotel room for a weekend, to a
country cabin, to anyplace where they can be by themselves.
When my father died, many of my old knots came untied. While
in the midst of loose ends, I drove up to my farm alone and lived
there for several days. I grieved. I recalled old memories. I
thought about my own mortality. For two days I wrote nearly
nonstop about what I had learned from my father. Slowly I began to feel better as I replaced old knots with new connections. I
am not finished. I am still working on the meaning of my father's
passing, but the old knots are gone forever.

Reconnecting

Beyond the phase of loose ends we begin to develop new
connections; we begin retying and reconnecting. Once we have
gone through a dramatic change, the nature of our new connections (knots) will not only be profoundly different from those
that came untied, but the nature of connection itself will be
different. Our knots will be more tentative; yet they will be
stronger. We also will expect them to become untied again and
again as we move through life. Thus, life becomes a series of untying, being at loose ends, and reconnecting.

None of us goes through a dramatic life change in the same
way. Many try to go directly from untying to reconnecting, trying to avoid the loose ends phase. When we do this, we miss an
opportunity to learn, as painful as the learning may be. Cleans-
ing takes place when we wrestle with the nothingness of not
knowing which way to turn, and of not knowing what we believe, or even not knowing what we know. From the depths of
unknowing comes something new and vital. From loose ends
come new connections, and new connections mean moving beyond where we have been to concern for where we are going.

EXERCISE 4.3   DRAMATIC LIFE CHANGES

- Select any event from your life that you believe resulted in a dramatic life change. Write the details of the event. Who or what was involved? What were the circumstances? Try to recall the feelings you had at that time.
- How do you believe what happened at that time influences your life today?
- How has your view of that event changed over the years? What are your feelings about that event today?

CHAPTER 5

Relationships

Learning from the heart means developing relationships with ourselves, nature, community, knowledge, and an entity outside ourselves. It means facing the mystery of relationships, of learning how to create them, and then of learning from them. Learning from the heart means experiencing the joy of relationships and the tragedy that sometimes results. It means accepting the hard work that relationships require and the constant attention they need for survival. There is no such thing as establishing a relationship and then ignoring it. An ignored relationship leads to a severed one.

DIFFICULTY IN ESTABLISHING RELATIONSHIPS

Establishing and maintaining relationships are difficult tasks, particularly in our society where independence and individualism are exalted.

Forty years ago, Erich Fromm (1956) wrote: "Modern man has transformed himself into a commodity; he experiences his life energy as an investment with which he should make the highest profit, considering his position and the situation on the personality market. He is alienated from himself, from his fellowmen, and from nature. His main aim is profitable exchange of his skills, knowledge, and of himself, his 'personality package' with others who are equally intent on a fair and profitable exchange. Life has no goal except the one to move, no principle except the one of fair exchange, no satisfaction except the one to consume"

(p. 88). Fromm made an important point that largely holds today. Along the same lines of total emphasis on the individual,
Robert Bellah and associates (1985) lamentably conclude that
"The individual is prior to society, which comes into existence
only through the voluntary contract of individuals trying to
maximize their own self-interest" (p. 143).

So learning from the heart, with its focus on relationships,
is challenged from the beginning. We all must confront this major icon of our society—individualism—and its resultant outcomes: excessive competition with winning at all cost and the accumulation of material goods as proof of success.

Even establishing internal relationships is resisted by our
busy, achievement-oriented society. Taking time to examine
who we are and what we believe and value is too often viewed as
frivolous, nonproductive, self-centered, and unimportant. As a
result, we have a lack of authentic relationships either internal or
external. The relationships we believe we have are often superficial and fleeting. We've all heard stories of people living for years
in a neighborhood and not knowing the names of their neighbors. At best there's a nod when people meet in the morning or
a "how are you" when they see each other carrying out the
garbage.

We can learn to develop deeper and more authentic relationships, an essential component in learning from the heart. As
we develop fuller, more thorough, and deeper relationships, we
learn from the process. We move from the narrow perspective
that learning must be always for something, in this case for improving relationships, to learning as a natural outcome of something occurring.

LEARNING FROM RELATIONSHIPS

Learning *from* relationships rather than learning *for* relationships is a difficult shift in thinking for many of us. We are so
accustomed to the idea that learning should have an external purpose that we have difficulty comprehending that learning, particularly learning that involves the whole person, can have value
in and of itself. Interestingly when we are less intent on learning

how to improve our relationships, and relax to learn from the relationships, the relationships often improve.

So often these days, we hear the comment that if the learning is not practical, why bother. It is bewildering for many people that the most profound learning they do may have no immediately recognizable outcome. Yet struggling with questions such as Who are we? What is our purpose for living? What is the meaning of our lives? stretches us and helps make us more human, helps give meaning to our lives, and helps us experience a depth of living. These struggles also help us as we reach out to others. The interplay of looking inward and acting outward, always in tension, can lead to further self-understanding. We wake up to what it means to be alive, what it means to be human. Such learning comes from our hearts.

DEVELOPING INTERNAL RELATIONSHIPS

Developing internal relationships means connecting ourselves to ourselves. It means connecting us to our intellectual, emotional, spiritual and physical selves. And it means connecting our various selves to each other, to comprise a whole rather than segments of relationships.

EXERCISE 5.1   LIFE CIRCLE

- Draw a circle and divide it into four parts.
- Label each of the sections: intellectual, emotional, spiritual, and physical.
- Place a dot in each quarter at the place that represents the amount of attention you give to this area; toward the outside is great, toward the inside suggests improvement is needed.
- Within the large circle, draw a circle that connects the dots.
- How lopsided is your life circle?
- Is your lopsided, inner circle much smaller than the outside circle?
- Consider what your inner circle looked like 5 years ago. Do you believe you gave less or more attention to each of the four dimensions of your life then?

- Draw a new circle with the four segments represented.
- Draw the inner circle representing the attention you wish to give to each of these areas within the next year.
- What barriers do you need to overcome to realize your second inner circle?

Connecting with Our Intellectual, Physical, and Emotional Selves

Most of us have had extensive experience connecting to our intellectual self. The more formal education we have, the more adept we are at linking to our thoughtful, rational, intellect. We have likely read about critical thinking approaches, learning styles, and other strategies designed to help cultivate our intellect. As part of our formal education, we have learned how to analyze and critically judge the work of others. It is all part of our intellectual training and experience.

Weight loss and physical fitness programs have become popular everywhere, an attention to our physical selves. Men and women are running and walking, lifting weights, working on ski machines, riding stationary bikes, and using a host of other exercise equipment in the name of physical fitness. Unfortunately, most of the attention doesn't focus so much on relating to our physical self as it assumes the body is a machine, a kind of taxi that carries around our intellect. It must be kept in "good shape" in order to do its task, and we take it for granted.

We are all aware of our emotions. We know anger, guilt, frustration, pleasure, fear, anxiety, joy, and disgust. But most of us do not know how to relate to our emotions. We know we have them, but we often try to ignore them. Our society discredits people who "can't control their emotions." A presidential candidate a few years ago was forced to drop from the race because he was seen crying. As a result of society's negative and stereotyped attitude toward expressing emotion (women can cry, men shouldn't), we try to avoid our emotions or hide them. Relating to our emotions is one way to learn from the heart.

Connecting with Our Hearts

Relating to our hearts (souls) is the most difficult of all the internal connections. Our souls are mysteries to us. We talk, jokingly sometimes, of losing our souls or of what it would take to save our souls. Or we say, "That person has lost her soul," or, "He has no soul." But we don't think much about what we are saying. At another level, we may discuss "soul food" or "soul music." For some of us, "soul talk" happens in religious institutions. Many more of us would concede that the soul is a part of who we are and that concern for it should not be left to formal religion.

When we connect with our hearts, we connect to the core of what makes us human. We move from the surface to the depths. In the tapestry that is our life, when we search for heart we look for the threads behind the threads—those that may be invisible but are vital, those that provide a backdrop and a foundation for the more colorful threads that are on the surface and greet the public.

Thomas Moore (1992), Alan Jones (1985), Jack Kornfield (1993), and others talk about various characteristics of soul (heart). To begin to know something about the soul is an entry toward developing a relationship with it.

Thomas Moore (1992) describes the power of the soul. He writes, "The power of the soul . . . is more like a great reservoir or, in traditional imagery, like the force of water in a fast rushing river" (p. 119).

The soul likes to deal with big problems. When it deals only with small, solvable problems, it shrivels. "Gigantic questions about love, death, power, and time feed the soul. They do not confront us as problems to be solved, but as mysteries to be wondered at, or intractable darkness to be raged at or endured" (Jones, 1985, pp. 134–135).

The soul (heart) requires time to contemplate, to consider matters in depth, to look beneath the surface, to explore, as Clarissa Pinkola Estes (1992) suggests, "the river beneath the river" (p. 9). The soul revels in layers of meaning, never content with a simple, quick answer, but not discounting that answer either as other answers are sought. The soul likes mystery and accepts ambiguity.

"The intellect often demands proof that it is on solid ground. The thought of the soul finds its grounding in a different way. It likes persuasion, subtle analysis, an inner logic, and elegance. It enjoys the kind of discussion that is never complete, which ends with a desire for further talk or reading. It is content with uncertainty and wonder. Especially in ethical matters, it probes and questions and continues to reflect even after decisions have been made" (Moore, 1992, pp. 245–246).

So developing a relationship with our hearts may require us to rethink how we think, to reconsider how we consider. The heart accepts that life consists of complementary opposites: yin and yang. "Yang is active, dynamic, assertive, yin is quiet, yielding, receptive. In nature, yin and yang combine patterns of highs and lows, mountains and valleys, turbulence and tranquility" (Dreher, 1990, p. 31). Other complementary opposites include science and art, creativity and discipline, rationality and intuitiveness, work and play, noise and quiet, city and country.

Developing a relationship to our heart, like all other relationships, requires attention and continual effort.

DEVELOPING EXTERNAL RELATIONSHIPS

Learning from the heart comprises much more than getting in touch with our inner nature and developing different aspects of self. Developing internal relations is an excellent place to start. It is difficult to develop external relationships without having done some work in developing internal ones. Of course, as we develop external relationships, we also further our inward look. As Paul Tillich (1948) wrote, "We are only in a world through a community of [people]. And we can discover our souls only through the mirror of those who look at us. There is no depth of life without the depth of the common life" (p. 57).

Relating to Community

To learn from the heart is to encourage the development of community. M. Scott Peck (1987) said it best when he wrote, "In

and through community lies the salvation of the world" (p. 17).
Later he wrote about how rare the community is these days. In
our quest for individualism and the accomplishment of self, we
overlook the power and the need for common experience. Community means living a common experience, sharing and caring,
and helping—and realizing that community *is more than the sum*
of those who make it up.

My introduction to community came early. Community
meant neighbors working together at harvesting time when we
threshed, filled silos, and harvested corn. Community meant attending church suppers, no matter which denomination spon-
sored it. Community meant knowing that help was only a phone
call away. Community was a sense of belonging and knowing
one's place. Community meant knowing our neighbors and
knowing them well.

We were at the same time free to be ourselves, to farm in the
way we wanted to farm, and yet we were ready to cooperate as
well. We talked about each other and joked about those who
made some error in planting a crop or repairing a farm imple-
ment. But it was in fun, not designed to exclude or embarrass. No
one was left out, not even the most eccentric. One of our neighbors was a thief. He stole grain and chickens and even wrenches
from machinery left in the field. We all knew this, yet we never
reported this person. We included him and his family in our social activities and our shared work projects. As neighbors go,
everyone considered him a good one because he was always
ready to help out (but we kept our best tools out of sight when
he was around).

Czech President Vaclav Havel provides a fundamental ar-
gument as to why community is important. "The earth is a
'mega-organism' on which all of us depend. . . .we are not here
alone nor for ourselves alone, but that we are an integral part of
higher, mysterious entities against which it is not advisable to
blaspheme" (cited in Woodward, 1994, p. 66).

Woodward, in examining the meaning of Havel's comments says, "In part, it was a bold assertion that the 18th-century
philosophy of individual rights—and the abstract deist divinity
from which it derived—has failed to nourish a sense of human
solidarity and social responsibility. He wants a shared global

vision that enables diverse people, multi-cultural societies and competing religions to transcend their particularities" (p. 66).

Community means much more than geographic areas. People of like minds can form communities; people who learn from the heart can become a community and share ideas and support each other using media as electronic mail and computer Internet connections. A few basic criteria seem important for communities to form and continue: people with something in common, a willingness to support each other, a concern for honesty and integrity, and a willingness to allow a community truth to emerge from the interactions, something larger than the sum of the members that make up the community.

Relating to community often means taking action in behalf of the community. People often believe that we relate to community only for our personal betterment. Learning from the heart can result in collective action and community change, as well as individual action and individual change. Only through community can we solve many environmental problems such as air and water pollution. Only through community can we address many of the social problems that affect our nation.

Developing a relationship with community means thinking beyond ourselves and our own needs, desires, and ambitions. It means learning how to think collectively and how to address and solve problems as a group.

Relating to Nature

One set of relationships often overlooked, ignored, or viewed as something nice but not essential is how we relate to the natural world. To realize that we, as human beings, are *of the natural world,* not apart from it is new thinking for some. To recognize the biology of our existence and the natural connections we have with all life forms, and indeed with all elements of the natural world, is what is required.

I recently had an extended conversation with a Native American friend who explained his beliefs about everything having a spirit, whether it is a rock, a tree, or an eagle soaring overhead. He told me how he believed his spirit was connected to all spirits existing in the world. Most people don't view connections to nature in this way. Loren Eiseley (1970) said that modern people have "... come to look upon nature as a thing outside [themselves]—an object to be manipulated or discarded at will" (p. 59).

We've come to see nature as a "resource," something that is there for our use, something to be consumed, rather than something of which we are a part. Most states in our country have departments of natural resources with responsibility for water, air, wild animals, forests, and minerals. The focus of these agencies is on best use, not on developing relationships.

To accept that we are a part of nature is a humbling act. We've been led to believe that we can control nature. We've tried with dams and dikes on our major rivers, buildings designed to resist earthquakes and strong winds, and a host of other attempts. Just when we think we have nature under control, a hurricane roars inland and destroys millions of dollars of property, or heavy rains cause rivers to flood thousands of acres.

Relating to nature means meeting nature on its terms, not our terms. Canoeing in the Boundry Waters of northern Minnesota renews my relationship with nature each year. I listen for the call of the loon echoing across a secluded lake. I watch a campfire, its flames licking at the twigs of wood I feed it. A sliver of smoke sifts through the tops of the birch and spruce trees that surround my campsite. I stare into the flames, as people for thousands of years have done. The flames jump and twist, turn from yellow to blue and back to yellow again. And as the twigs are consumed, the flames slowly die and the remaining coals shimmer in the blackness of night where there is no electricity for 50 miles.

I watch a bank of clouds in the west slowly come closer. Sometime in the night I awaken to the sound of raindrops on canvas, and I hear the low growl of thunder in the distance. As the storm comes closer, the thunder rolls across the lake and tumbles onto the shore, sometimes shaking the ground beneath my tent. Lightning cuts through the blackness of the night, illuminating the inside of the tent for a brief moment before total blackness again. It is like someone turning on and off a bright lightbulb.

Canoe-camping in the Boundary Waters is one way for me to connect with the natural world, to keep me humble in face of the vastness of what we call nature.

RELATIONSHIPS AMONG RELATIONSHIPS

Developing relationships with community and with nature are but examples of the many relationships that are a part of learning from the heart. Relating to knowledge and relating to the divine being are other examples that we could explore.

As our inward relationships connect to each other, so do our outward relationships. Ideas from relating to community fit within our relationship to nature, and vice versa.

And, as we develop our external relationships, we find them connecting to our internal relationships. For instance, as I sit staring into the campfire flames, I feel the depths of who I am and find yet another dimension of my heart. My relationship to nature is enhancing my exploration of self.

Learning from the heart is relationship, not a technique for developing relationship. Learning from the heart reaches new levels when all of the relationships come together.

Part II

Teaching from the Heart

CHAPTER 6

The Core of Who We Are

Teaching from the heart means teaching from the depths of who we are with the hope that we will touch the hearts of those with whom we work. To begin discovering the core of who we are requires that we work to become aware of our beliefs and values.

BELIEFS AND VALUES

A belief is what we accept as truth. Others may not agree, yet our beliefs are our truths. For example, we may believe that people are inherently good. Our neighbor may believe just the opposite, that people are inherently bad and must be controlled.

Values are principles that guide us and give us a sense of direction, that help us decide what is important and provide us with an ethical and moral foundation. Concern for the environment is a value. Another value is giving children the best possible care.

Our beliefs and values, largely, influence what we do and how we do it, even what we see and how we see it. In other words, our beliefs and values are a basis for who we are as teachers and influence greatly how we teach. Following is an exercise to help you identify beliefs and values about your teaching.

EXERCISE 6.1   EXAMINING BELIEFS AND VALUES

1. On the top of a blank sheet of paper write, "When I teach I . . ." Write statements that describe your present teaching.

2. Once you have developed a list, sit back and consider what beliefs and values lie beneath your statements. If you are doing
this exercise in a group, or even with one other person, share
your list and encourage this person to write what beliefs and
values seem foundational to your statements about teaching.

In response to question 1, teachers in my workshops have written—When I teach:

- I am in control.
- I make sure I know my subject matter.
- I try to make my presentations clear.
- I challenge participants to think.
- I often use humor.
- I make sure my classes are well planned, and I stick to my plan,
avoiding sidetracks and distractions.

In response to question 2, teachers wrote the following belief
and value statements:

- It is important for a group to stay on track, and it is my responsibility to keep them pointed in the right direction.
- People learn best when they are clear about what it is they are ex-
pected to learn.
- I am responsible for the subject matter that students will learn.
- I have responsibility for knowing ahead of time what each class
period should accomplish and then not deviate from the plan.
- Learning can be fun, and interjecting a little humor is one way to
do it.

As you realize from earlier chapters in this book, some of these
belief and value statements are consistent with learning from the
heart, and some are not. Statements, 1, 3, and 4, for instance, are
about teacher control, not about shared learning where everyone is
a teacher and everyone is a learner. Belief statements 2 and 5 are
more consistent with the premises of learning from the heart.

You may want to compare your belief and value statements
with the premises of learning from the heart (Chapter 1). Do you see
a need to change?

EXAMINING THE CORE

Examining our beliefs and values about teaching is essential, but there is more to examining our cores. We must go deeper. As we explore the depths of who we are, we often begin touching our souls or our hearts. In the darkness of who we are is a light that guides us, a compass that shows the way, yet gives us an individuality that makes us different from everything and everyone else. It is the heart of who we are.

Many believe we only should talk about heart in religious institutions. Mention the word in everyday conversation and some conclude that we are avoiding the practical, everyday concerns of life. How unfortunate. By not getting in touch with our hearts, we bypass a fundamental dimension of who we are and what guides us. As I have written earlier, each of us is a whole person who thinks, has emotions, has a physical body, and has *a soul or heart*. We cannot be whole if we avoid the heart or segregate its care to those brief moments when we enter a house of worship. We cannot teach from the heart if we avoid recognizing and nurturing the deeper dimensions of who we are.

KNOWING OUR HEARTS

Thomas Moore (1992) says, "'Soul' [heart] is not a thing, but a quality or dimension of experiencing life and ourselves. It has to do with depth, value, relatedness, heart, and personal substance" (p. 5). Getting in touch with our hearts means paying attention to what is occurring in our lives, "listening" to all of our senses, and immersing ourselves in the experience of the moment.

Sometimes we get in touch with our hearts in moments of stress and hardship, or when we're seriously ill. When I was 12 years old, I contracted polio, a dangerous, frightful disease that killed several of my friends and left others far more impaired than I. It came unexpectedly. One day I was fine, helping my father with farm chores, walking to school, and playing softball with my friends. A week later my right leg was paralyzed and I couldn't walk. As I learned about the disease and what to expect from it, a great sense of loss swept over me. This meant the end of softball, skiing, squirrel hunting, and walking in the woods in summer, looking for blackberries, or not looking for much of anything, just walking and enjoying the warm weather and the coolness under the oaks.

For six months my right knee was frozen at a 45 degree angle. Slowly and painfully, I began to walk again, one difficult, painful step at a time. But I couldn't run after that, couldn't even walk fast without falling on my face. I became a frail, sickly kid that some thought was destined to become an observer rather than a participant.

Today, as I reflect on that experience, I remember months of feeling sorry for myself, of not being able to do the physical things my friends could do. But while I was unable to do much physically, I read everything I could get my hands on. And I spent a lot of time thinking. I'm sure I wasn't aware of it then, but I was in touch with the depths of who I was as I asked the often asked question of people in my circumstance, "Why me?"

To confront one's mortality at age 12 is not something I would wish on anyone, yet the confrontation pushed me toward discovering what was important in my life. I came to appreciate the capabilities I had and my need to develop them as well as I could. I thought about an external being and how what had happened to me perhaps was meant to happen. This I haven't yet resolved in my mind.

My physical impairment became a window to my heart. I can say it now with considerable confidence, for the decisions I made at that time and in the months and years following influenced my life profoundly. Never again did I take my health for granted.

Getting in touch with our hearts need not result from something painful. It can be a personal high, a "peak experience." For me, standing on the top of a hill on my farm, on a summer evening, with the sun sinking below the horizon provides such an experience. No two evenings are the same, yet each one *is* the same. The panorama of color changes with each sunset, but the feelings I have are similar. I am relaxed and feel fully alive. I hear the last calls of the songbirds in the trees back of me as they prepare for an evening of rest. In the distance, in the deep woods to the north, I often hear the hoot of an owl and sometimes the gobble of a wild turkey. In springtime I may hear a ruffed grouse drumming. I try to attend to all the sights, sounds, and smells as the evening coolness quiets the excitement of the day and wisps of fog rise from the meadows with a sweet, subtle evening smell.

EXERCISE 6.2   GETTING IN TOUCH
WITH YOUR HEART

- Recall one or more times where you believe you were in touch with your heart.
- Describe the experience in as much depth as you can. Were other people present? Did they have a similar experience?
- What is your personal definition of heart?
- What did it feel like to be in touch with your heart?
- What thoughts have you had about the experience?
- Have you been able to repeat the experience?

Even when we are able to get in touch with our hearts, we're reluctant to act on what we are discovering. The whole idea of teaching from the heart, beyond the superficial, may be new to us and we don't know how to proceed. The use of *affirmations* can help. Affirmations are positive statements of belief that serve as a foundation for our action. Shakti Gawain (1978) says, "An affirmation is a strong, positive statement that something is already so. It is a way of 'making firm' that which you are imaging" (p. 21).

When you first look at the sample list below, you may say the statements sound syrupy and unrealistic for busy people in a hard-nosed, practical, and highly competitive world. But look out, for there is great power in affirmations. You've all heard the statement, "Be careful about what you dream for, for your dreams are likely to come true."

When you first write an affirmation, especially if they are similar to those I include below, you inner censor will begin working overtime, telling you just how dumb the statement sounds. Confront this demon censor if this occurs. Why such an outcry? The affirmations you write that evoke the most negative responses may very well be the most important ones for you. But you'll never know until you begin writing them. Here are some examples for you to mull over:

- I nurture my heart and it in turn nurtures me.
- Being in touch with my heart is healing for me and for others.
- As I listen to my heart, I am led by it.
- Being in touch with my heart leads to my truth.
- My dreams come from my heart, and my heart allows them to happen.
- Being in touch with my heart allows for self-forgiveness and the forgiveness of others.
- I am in touch with my heart, and I allow my teaching to flow from it.

VISITING OUR HISTORIES

Much of who we are today, what we believe and value, and how we behave is a product of our histories. Few have taken the time to visit their histories and discover some of what has shaped them.

EXERCISE 6.3   A FLOOR PLAN TO YOUR HISTORY

- Draw a detailed floor plan of your house or apartment when you were 10.
- Include the furniture in the rooms; note the pictures on the wall, the people in the rooms, the smells, sounds, and feelings.
- Describe your house as a novelist might, relating in some detail what is there, evoking as many of the senses as possible.
- What feelings are associated with each room?
- Spend sometime reflecting on your drawing.
  -Are your feelings today the same as they were then?
  -What do these early experiences mean for you now?
  -Are there life themes, behaviors, and feelings that echoed in these experiences and that you confront today?
  -How are these experiences a mirror of you today?

-How do you integrate this child into the person you are today?
-What parts do you hold on to, exclude, hide?
-What values did you have then that are still present?
-What did you believe then that you continue to believe today?

Family Rules of Conduct

We acquire many of our beliefs and values in our growing up years. Often, we are not even aware of the beliefs and values we are getting. Much of who we are today, how we think, how we react to situations, what we do, and what we avoid doing is influenced greatly by these early experiences. In many instances our parents passed on to us what they had learned from their parents. Thus, family lines develop their own cultures. How often do you say something to your child and then stop and recall that your parents said the same words in the same tone of voice?

The voices of our parents, preachers, teachers, and relatives are in our heads, telling us what to do and not to do, what to believe and not to believe, what to value and not to value. These voices greatly influenced our early learning—they shaped us to fit the cultural situation of which we were a part.

For instance, my childhood family had several rules for living. Here are some examples.

Be on time. Not being on time was as serious an offense as lying. The clocks in our house were 15 minutes ahead to assure that we were always at least 15 minutes early for appointments. When we attended church, we were at least a half-hour ahead of time; when we visited a relative who had said come at 6:00 p.m., we arrived at 5:45.

As a child, stay in the background. Adults are important, children less so.

City people are important, farm people are not (we were farm people). No matter if you were a child or an adult, in the presence of city people you deliberately stayed in the background. Those with less education remained in the background to those with more education.

Like so many rules of this sort, there were many paradoxes and contradictions as well. Although we were taught to stay in the background to those who lived in the city and to those who had more education, that didn't prevent us from poking fun at "city slickers" and "book-learned fools." In our quiet way, when not in the presence of these people, we expressed our superiority over them.

Know your place. This meant never eating at a fancy restaurant, never saying hello to someone wearing a suit unless they spoke first, never buying anything that was expensive such as clothing, furniture, and appliances, especially if a less expensive and often lower quality item was available.

Hard work solves all problems. If you confront some difficulty and it is not easily solved, work harder and you will solve it. This strategy applied to all problems ranging from moving a large stone from a cornfield, to resolving a conflict with a neighbor.

Save your money. No matter how small your salary, save some of it.

There are many more "rules for living" that I could list from my childhood. Many of them I have learned to ignore or have modified to fit today's situation. But some of these guidelines continue to influence me, sometimes without my awareness. For example, no matter what appointment I have, I make sure that I am never late. Too often, I am embarrassed at being the first one to some social event or to some committee meeting where it didn't matter if I was on time.

EXERCISE 6.4   VOICES FROM YOUR PAST

What voices do you hear that tell you what to do and what not to do, what to believe and not believe, what to value and not value?

- List ten rules for living for your family. Were any of the rules I listed above present in your family? Be particularly mindful of rules that you believe were unique to your family.
- Did you turn up rules that you haven't thought about or considered for many years? Which ones?
- How have you modified any of these rules today? Which rules have you tried to ignore, and find it difficult to do so?

• Which of these family rules are an integral part of your present day belief and value system?

Community Rules

Just as families have rules that are passed on to its members, so do communities or collections of families that interact. In my rural neighborhood, we knew our neighbors well and depended on them greatly. Each of these families had its own history and its own rules. Our rural neighborhood included families of German, Polish, English, Welsh, and Norwegian backgrounds. They were Methodist, Baptist, Lutheran, Catholic, and at least one family that never attended church and thought churches were nonsense and a waste of time.

Just as I learned from my family a set of rules for conduct, I learned still other rules from the neighbors who lived around us. Some of these were:

• It didn't matter if people attended church or not, they were still our neighbors and important to us.
• Being German didn't mean that I was less or more important than those representing other immigrant groups.
• If a neighbor had a problem and asked for help, we would drop everything and help that neighbor.

You may find it useful to reflect on the community rules for conduct that you recall from your youth. Which of these guide you today? Which ones have you reflected on and then rejected?

KNOWN AND UNKNOWN BELIEFS AND VALUES

Some of our beliefs and values are public and we freely share them. Others are private and we keep them to ourselves. Many of our beliefs and values are hidden. We don't know what they are, yet they influence how we relate to other people as profoundly as if we were aware of them. One of the challenges of getting in touch with our hearts is to uncover some of these hidden beliefs and values. Did any emerge as you worked through the exercises in this chapter?

To teach from the heart, we must first explore the core of who we are. Then we are ready to go on and develop teaching strategies that will assist others learn from the heart, the subject of the next and succeeding chapters.

CHAPTER 7

Paradoxes and a Credo

Teaching from the heart means working beneath the river that runs through our lives, and helping others to get in touch with their undercurrents. Approaches for teaching from the heart lie beneath the approaches we ordinarily use. To teach from the heart means going deeper, searching for the core of things.

We appreciate and encourage learning that occurs beyond our classes, workshops, and conferences. Rather than thinking of all learning as linear, from the discussion in Chapter 4, we can see much of it as cyclic. We all return periodically to themes we have earlier confronted, such as developing relationships, searching for meaning, exploring creativity, confronting mortality, revisiting personal histories, and working toward self-knowledge. We have experienced this in our own learning. It is likely that most of those who participate in our teaching are experiencing these cycles as well. As life themes are revisited, we all will face dramatic life changes from time to time, transitions in our lives that point us in new directions, with new beliefs and sometimes even new or modified values.

As teachers, we are constantly exploring our beliefs and values, with the expectation that our teaching will encourage those in contact with us to do so, too. Getting in touch with our hearts is one critical dimension of this exploration.

To teach from the heart means attending to relationships, those within us and those outside us. Another outcome of teaching from the heart is to encourage learners to explore their own internal relationships as well as those involving community, nature, and knowledge.

A critical relationship for the teacher is with learners. This relationship is one that must be constantly explored, examined, nourished and, celebrated. We don't establish such a relationship once and then assume that it will continue. Like all other relationships, this one requires constant attention and hard work.

GUIDELINES FOR GROUPS

When teaching from the heart, several guidelines can assist in making the experience a positive and meaningful one for participants.

Learning Environment

William Draves (1994) talks about the need for "learning mediums" to enhance learning. He writes, "Learning mediums occupy the middle ground between the presenter and the participant. They often surround or envelop the participant. Sometimes they are the substance through which an effect is transmitted" (p. 105). Draves says the learning environment can be enhanced through the use of flowers, music, refreshments, and a comfortable room, including how the room is arranged. Sometimes we forget how important these things are for learning, and particularly for the development of a group.

Most of us know what wonderful discussions take place during the breaks in classes and workshops. Especially for a new group, breaks provide a chance for people to get to know each other that goes well beyond what happens during the more formal sessions.

Psychological Safety

Beyond physical comfort, psychological safety is also important. Breaks, flowers, music, and room arrangements contribute to psychological comfort, but we must also be concerned with psychological safety. As we attempt to teach from the heart and encourage participants to learn from the heart, we need to provide an environment that encourages participants and teachers to share openly and trust each other, particularly during times when the learner may be uncomfortable with the learning.

Psychological safety includes teacher and participant interactions. It also includes the nature of interactions among students. I once attended a creative writing class where the norm was that students criticized each other's work unmercifully, to the point that many participants were reluctant to share their material. The teacher's attitude was that people must learn how to accept criticism. This is certainly a reasonable expectation within any class or workshop. But it is the way in which the criticism is offered that makes all the difference. Many find it easier to critique in a mean-spirited, "I can top you" style that tears down rather than builds up. Critique can be offered in a loving, caring way, and be gladly and openly accepted.

Playfulness in a group also contributes to psychological safety and to deeper learning. Baud and Griffin (1987) say, "A playful approach to learning helps us engage and connect with parts of ourselves which are usually dormant, inaccessible, or not well defined. In the process we shuffle, sort and arrange the various images and symbols which have been stored from life's experiences" (p. 17). We tend to take ourselves too seriously most of the time. Drawing, using three-dimensional materials, described below, and story sharing can lead to playfulness.

GROUND RULES

Teachers and participants together have the responsibility for establishing the ground rules early in a class or workshop—particularly those that will meet for several times. Some of these ground rules could include:

1. Everyone agrees on the direction the group is headed. The direction the group takes may change as the discussion proceeds, but the teacher and participants decide on the change.

2. It is vital to listen to what the other person is saying.
3. Everyone who wants to say something is allowed that opportunity.
4. Those who wish to remain silent, for whatever reason, have that right.
5. Participants should never do anything or say anything that they are not comfortable saying or doing.
6. Expressions of emotion should not be criticized but embraced.
7. Abusive criticism is not allowed. Abusive criticism is that which demeans, ridicules, or condemns, and it is often personally directed.

UNEXPECTED OUTCOMES

It occurs rarely, but it does happen, that when some persons begin getting in touch with themselves they uncover more than they can handle, even with group support. When this occurs, our challenge is not to take on the healing of this person, but to encourage the person to seek professional help.

This does not mean that the first time you see tears or anger you should assume that a person needs professional help. Tears and anger are often a natural expression of joy as well as unhappiness. When do you know to encourage someone to seek professional help? Most know themselves when to do so. Others will, with a bit of encouragement, and perhaps some suggestions of where to turn.

In my workshops and courses, I provide a variety of safety nets for participants who do not want to explore areas they find too disturbing or deal with issues they have met before and with which they had difficulty. Participants always have choices. They can choose how much or how little to participate. They can choose when to respond to a question and when not to respond. For instance, when I ask people to share from their journals, I always say that they should never share anything they are not comfortable sharing. Journal writing itself is a type of safety net for people who want to explore deeply some personal issues, but may not, at least at that time, want others to know what they are wrestling with.

Having clear choices for participants keeps teaching from the heart an educational activity and helps to prevent it from straying into the realm of group therapy.

PARADOXES OF TEACHING FROM THE HEART

Teaching from the heart includes appreciating and even looking for paradoxes in our work. Accepting paradoxes is a characteristic of teaching from the heart that makes it different from more traditional approaches to teaching where paradox, uncertainty, and ambiguity are avoided if at all possible.

Some of the paradoxes of teaching from the heart include:

- The question is often the answer—our questions, and those of our participants.
- To become comfortable alone, we join a group.
- To be ourselves we must be alone; to be ourselves we must be with others.
- The more things change the more they remain the same.
- We teach more by teaching less.
- To the extent we help individuals in their development, we help our own development.
- We move beyond categories so we can see the value of categories.
- We discover our own individuality as we develop stronger relationships with those we teach.
- We learn how to teach ourselves so we can better teach others.
- We maintain our consistency as teachers as we constantly change.
- We live in the present so we can benefit from the past and be guided by the future.
- We center on maturity and applaud a childlike nature.
- We seek certainty and mystery, fact and fable, poetry and prose—simultaneously.
- We promote solitude and community.
- We work less hard and accomplish more.
- We seek moments of stability in order to face chaos.
- We slow down and cover a greater distance.

- We accept that learning occurs in cycles and in straight lines.
- We plan our teaching and applaud what occurs beyond our planning.
- When we lose we gain, when we gain we lose.
- We plan our teaching and take advantage of the spontaneity of the moment.
- Every ending is a beginning.

LEARNING DURING CRISIS

To teach from the heart means facing crisis and attempting to learn from it. Most of us do not plan for a crisis. Crises sneak up on us, like fog in the valley on a clear summer night. Not long ago my father died at age 93.

Growing up on a farm, I learned to know my father well. I was the oldest son, and as I grew older I worked side by side with him in the hayfields and cornfields, in the cattle barn and chicken house, in summer and in winter. We worked together daily as we trudged to the barn each early morning and evening to milk our small herd of dairy cows.

After I moved off the farm, I returned regularly to help with farm work I had left behind. Sitting with my father that July evening, when he was dying, these memories flashed through my mind. My father had always been a quiet voice to offer me another perspective, another view. I didn't always agree with him, but he didn't seem to mind.

Upon his death my world was shaken—much more than I thought it would be. It was clearly a crisis. Part of me said I should learn from this. Another loud voice said, work hard and you'll forget and all of this will go away, after all, "time heals."

A quiet, muffled voice from deep inside whispered, get in touch with your grief and allow yourself to grieve the loss of your father. I grieved. As I did, I started a process of learning that will continue for some time.

As a part of grieving, I wrote in my journal, "Things I learned from my father." There are pages of memories, pages of learning that I seldom had thought about, indeed in some instances didn't even know I had. Some examples of what I remembered and wrote, often in the voice of my father:

- When you work, work hard and do the best job you are capable of doing. When you work for someone else, always do more than is asked. Come to work earlier than required and stay a little later.
- Exchange work with a neighbor, but don't worry about exchanging money. If your neighbor helps you for a half day, expect to help him for a half day. It doesn't matter what the task. Don't worry if you believe a half day of chopping wood is worth more than a half day of shocking grain. In the end it will all work out, and you will continue to have good neighbors.
- Always be available to help others, especially if they are your neighbors. Try to do more for others than they do for you.

This is the beginning of a long list that is growing ever longer. In the process of remembering this "learning," I am trying to recall, in some depth, both the facts and the feelings of my early years. There is joy in this activity, and great sorrow as well. But through this effort I am learning at a level that I have never before experienced. The death of my father became the stimulus for this learning, and though the process has been painful, I believe I am now a different person.

I have met persons in my workshops who avoid recalling the hurtful things in their lives. They sweep them aside, try to bury them, ignore them, or work ever harder at their jobs in the belief that somehow the hurt will go away. It doesn't. It hangs on, like a black cloud over our heads, ready to dump cold rain on us at the most unsuspecting time. Though it hurts, deeply and profoundly, the sad times in our lives can be times for great learning.

L. Robert Keck (1992) wrote, "When we face a crisis, do we focus only on the danger, and circle the wagons, or do we recognize and take advantage of the opportunities, no matter how dangerous they may be? Crises, and the transitional times they provide, present us with both danger and opportunities" (p. 92). The danger rests in what we uncover when we began confronting parts of our self we have never confronted. We may turn up more work than we bargained for.

Sometimes it takes the death of a loved one, the loss of a job, or a serious illness to shake us loose, to force us to pay attention to our own lives, where they have been and where they are going, who we've been and who we've become. Our challenge is to face the hurt head on. As Keck (1992) says, "If we can look beyond the dread of a situation, we can see with sacred eyes the disorganization that always precedes reintegration, the destruction that precedes restructuring, the breakdown that precedes break through, the death that precedes a rebirth, the endings that precede beginnings, and the night that precedes the dawn of a new day" (p. 97).

EXERCISE 7.1
RECALLING A HURTFUL EXPERIENCE

- Recall a recent hurtful experience.
- Describe it.
- Did you try to avoid confronting the experience? How?
- Were you conscious of your learning at the time?
- What pushed you into considering it enough so that you could start learning from it?
- What did you learn from the experience?
- Can you still learn more from this situation? What can you do to assure more learning?

FEAR OF LEARNING

Often, it is within feelings that we begin to learn at a deeper, more profound level. The exploration of feelings allows us to learn at ever deeper levels as more dimensions of feelings emerge. For some people in my workshops, the exploration of feelings is a taboo—something inappropriate to do as a part of learning. They use this excuse as a reason for not going deeper into their learning and for avoiding what they might uncover. Others are afraid to name their feelings for they fear what they will discover about themselves and their relationships to others. Uncovering feelings is new to many of us. It takes practice.

One way to avoid the fear of learning with the heart is to keep everything at arms length, not to put "you" into your learning. Our schooling, in most instances, has taught us how to do this, how to remain "objective" in our learning.

We read about Civil War history and memorize the dates of the great events: the Battle of Bull Run (1861), Gettysburg (1863), Sherman's march through Georgia (1864). We gather some details of the battles, the weapons used, the numbers of soldiers on each side, the numbers who were wounded, and the numbers who died. But we stop with that. We take an examination, receive our grade, and move on. If we earned a good grade, we are pleased with our learning, as are others.

When we learn from the heart, we go deeper. We explore our personal connection to this war. Perhaps a distant relative fought in it. We explore our feelings about the carnage; we consider the sounds of battle, the explosions of the cannons and the screams of the wounded. We envision the smells hanging in the air, one moment the smells of the countryside and the next the smells of destruction and death. We allow our feelings to emerge, feelings of rage, of compassion, of fear, of revulsion. Now we begin to learn about war at another level, a level that goes beyond the facts of the matter and begins touching on the feelings. We begin to learn as a whole person, not merely as a machinelike creature absorbing information to be recalled on some examination. In the process of going deeper we sometimes turn up thoughts and perspectives that scare us. We wonder about their source, and think that had we not probed deeper, these troublesome thoughts might not have emerged.

Many learners fear bringing themselves into their learning. But as Dreher (1990) points out, "Only by facing our fears do we recapture the emotional energy they absorb, the energy that otherwise imprisons us" (p. 59).

Unfortunately some teachers criticize learners who want to personalize what they are learning and who attempt to face their fears in the process—a sad commentary on education. Tying who we are to our learning can be a fearful thing, when we don't know what to expect and when we turn up something unpleasant. Yet, at the times when we are fearful and feel vulnerable and unsure, we are open to learning from the heart.

SEEKING SOLITUDE AND COMMUNITY

Solitude *and* community are both necessary for teaching and learning from the heart. Helping learners (and ourselves) appreciate the importance of both these dimensions is one of the challenges we face as teachers.

Most of us have little time alone and when we are alone we are lonely. We are often in the company of others, but seldom are we in true community where we, as a collective of human beings, can learn and grow together without concerns for besting each other, feeling inadequate or out of place, or believing that some external purpose must always result when groups of people come together. Often an external purpose will result such as collectively solving a community problem. But solving a community problem is not a requirement for community. A community can at times *just be.* It is comparable to a person *just being* and not always concerned with *doing something.*

Community allows us to be more than we can be as individuals. Community allows us to face the world as a collective rather than alone. We must rediscover the power of community, the joy of working and playing and living together, the wonder of collective action.

We must also rediscover the power of solitude. Solitude can help us examine the depths of who we are, in our own way and in our own time. Solitude can connect us with our creative self. As Anthony Storr (1988) writes, "The capacity to be alone . . . becomes linked with self-discovery and self-realization: with becoming aware of one's deepest needs, feelings, and impulses" (p. 21).

But it is not either-or. Community is not more important than solitude, nor is solitude more important than community. It is like asking which is more important—darkness or light, winter or summer, or men or women. Both are critical. Neither solitude nor community can be authentic without the other.

A CREDO FOR TEACHING FROM THE HEART

Following are several statements that I believe can serve as a foundation for the teacher who wishes to teach from the heart.

- We know our strengths and weaknesses and act on them. We are comfortable with ourselves and accept learners' strengths and weaknesses.
- We encourage, help, challenge, and implore learners to become comfortable with their own learning and the power of it. When learning comes from a person's heart and returns there, no one can shake this person into believing that the learning is unimportant. "If you are not afraid of the voice inside you, you will not fear the critics outside you" (Goldberg, 1986, p. 17).
- We believe that our relationship with learners is essential and special and that love and trust are embedded in it.
- As part of the relationship with learners, we accept that everyone is a teacher as well as a learner. We encourage learners to become teachers of others and of themselves.
- We are patient with learners. We give learners time and space to wrap their minds and emotions around their ideas. "Time is one of the most neglected topics in discussion of human relations. It takes a long time to make a soul" (Jones, 1985, p. 132).
- We know and trust our feelings. We attend to our feelings and do not attempt to push them aside, cover them up, or act as if we didn't have them.
- We consciously practice building relationships to our hearts.
- We are open to diverse perspectives, realizing that our truth is but one of many truths that exist in the world.
- We are aware that we have choices. The rules and regulations, the policies and traditions may force us to teach in a certain way, yet we have learned to look further and deeper.
- We accept that learning is much more than the gathering of other people's information and the development of particular skills.
- We leave room for mystery in our lives and the lives of others.
- We accept that our beliefs and values influence what we do and how we do it, even though we may never be totally aware of what we believe and value.
- We know that teaching from the heart comes from deep within us, that how we teach is unique to who we are, and that our teaching is an expression of our specialness as a human being.
- We have learned to listen to our hearts, for our hearts represent the depth of who we are.

CHAPTER 8

Personal Approaches

As mentioned earlier, the teaching approaches I am suggesting for learning from the heart are not meant to replace traditional teaching such as lecturing, small group discussion, and distance learning. Rather, they go beyond. The approaches suggested in this chapter are personal. Learners do them on their own. But as teachers from the heart, we have responsibility for informing learners about them.

CLEARING THE MIND

We all need to calm down and slow down. We need to calm the turmoil in our mind, to squelch the thoughts that ricochet around our heads, bouncing here and there and everywhere. We must quiet the rage in our minds, the torrent of new thoughts that cause us to scream out—"enough, enough." Yet we constantly search for more. Perhaps we are afraid that to face a calm, clear mind might be more devastating than confronting the usual clutter.

And we must slow down, become more deliberate, more aware of what is happening with us and around us. When we speed through life, we see only blurs, or the largest and the gaudiest billboards that scream for our attention. We hurry from appointment to appointment, from assignment to assignment, and at day's end we fall into a chair, exhausted. We have been everywhere and nowhere, we have accomplished much and we have accomplished nothing.

The Clearing is found in northern Door County, Wisconsin, along a cliff hanging over the blue waters of Green Bay. The

Clearing is an adult school of discovery in the arts, nature, and humanities. To enter the school grounds, we travel a narrow, twisty gravel road through a dense forest until, after we are quite sure we've missed a turn somewhere, we come upon a small field sprinkled with wildflowers. Surely this is how this place got its name we assume as we continue to the rustic stone lodge and the log and stone cabins.

Later we learn that landscape architect Jens Jensen had a different reason for naming the school as he did. He believed that each of us regularly must clear the mind of the world's clutter, and The Clearing is a place to do it.

I have led writing workshops at The Clearing for several years. Sitting high on a cliff above Green Bay, I feel the gentle westerly breeze that stirs the water and caresses the rocks below me. The sound is relaxing and mind clearing. A white cedar tree clinging to the edge of the cliff provides shade from the afternoon sun. An aspen tree's fan-shaped leaves nervously stutter, offering a counterpoint to the wave action below.

In the distance a single-masted sail boat cuts swiftly but silently through the water. Here is a place to clear my mind. Here is where I and many others come each year to focus on some task—write a short story, paint a picture, weave a rug—and discover deeper meaning in life.

As participants clear their minds and relax and begin getting in touch with themselves again, they begin to learn at deeper levels. They begin to touch the spiritual in their lives; they begin to communicate with their hearts. The classes they take are but vehicles, doorways to deeper learning. The place, with its abundance of wildflowers and songbirds, water and rocky shores, trees and meadows, is another doorway to the soul.

We must learn to clear our minds before such learning can occur. Sitting on a cliff with water pounding below is one way. Meditating is another. Praying works for some. A simple exercise I introduce to workshop participants involves breathing. I tell them to breathe deeply, hold their breath for an instant, and then breathe out. As they breathe, I ask them to say, "in," to themselves. When they breathe out, say, "out." In, out. Most of them are astounded how effective this is.

EXERCISE 8.1   A RELAXATION TECHNIQUE

One way to clear your mind is to learn how to relax.

- In a comfortable chair, sit up straight with your feet on the floor and your hands at your side or folded on your lap.
- Close your eyes and breathe deeply.
- Concentrate on the space within your big toe. Allow no other thoughts to interfere. Do this until you can feel this space. Sometimes you may also experience a tingling in your toe.
- Once you are able to do this, concentrate on the space within your ankles.
- Continue by concentrating on the space within your calves, thighs, buttocks, stomach, chest, shoulders, neck, and head.
- When you have proceeded through your body, concentrate on your personal space within all of space.
- Open your eyes and feel totally relaxed.

At first, this exercise may take you 15 minutes or longer to complete. Later, after you have done it a few times you'll be able to do it in 5 minutes or so. It is an excellent exercise to do prior to working on some activity that requires your entire attention.

There are other techniques for clearing your mind. "Feel the healing sensation of silence" says Dreher (1990, p. 80). During a busy day, find a place and time when you can be alone and it is quiet. Take a walk at lunch time, find time to watch a sunset, walk in the rain, observe birds at a feeder.

CONCENTRATION

These days most of us try to do a half dozen things at the same time. Even when we're "relaxing," we watch TV and read the newspaper, and sometimes even try to carry on a conversation all at the same time. Of course we don't do any of it well.

People accuse us of not listening, we end up skimming the newspaper, and we often are into the paper when the important news we want to see is on the screen. Our defense is that we don't have time to concentrate on things one at a time.

Many of us have lost the ability to concentrate—to dig deeply into some topic or activity and stay with it long enough to move beyond its superficial dimensions. Keck (1992) says ". . . education would serve us better if basic skills like concentration were taught rather than just learning facts that soon change or are out of date" (p. 210).

Teaching from the heart means helping learners move to the realization of who they are in relation to what they are studying. Sherman Stratford (1994) suggests one way to do this is to focus on the question. He says, "The ability to live in the question, rather than drive for the answer, helps you keep the antennae up and the eyes open" (p. 93).

"Living in the question" means taking time to focus on the moment, to dig deeply, to probe, to explore, to reflect, to uncover, to accept everything that turns up, at least for a time. Our tendency is to immediately begin sorting and discarding, and in the process we often toss away some of "the good stuff" without knowing we are doing it. The new perspective, the new insight, the new approach may emerge from what we initially considered the dregs of our inquiry.

In almost paradoxical fashion, Bateson (1994) reminds us that we must also learn to focus on more than one thing at the same time. She writes, "My life has forced me to adopt multiple levels of focus, shifting back and forth and embedding one activity within the other, parent and observer; teacher and student. I have been fortunate in living several lives simultaneously, the effect of layers of commitment" (p. 96).

Through concentration we are able to center ourselves, to keep ourselves in touch with who we are and what is important for us to think about and act upon. Richard Bode (1993), using the metaphor of sailing, says, "I see people all about me who have never developed an adequate inner clock and who are never at one with the wind because of it. The frantic individual tacks too soon, jumping from job to job, friendship to friendship, spouse to spouse, losing headway at every turn. The obtuse individual remains on the same tack too long, investing too much time, talent and energy in a course that takes him far from his avowed objective. But the seasoned sailor stays on the same tack as long as it appears advantageous, and then, at the appropriate moment, pushes the tiller toward the sail and deftly changes direction" (pp. 50–51).

Thus our challenge is to focus and at the same time to keep a broader perspective. Learning means maintaining a constant tension between focusing on the specific and maintaining a concern for broader, often more abstract ideas.

EXERCISE 8.2   CONCENTRATION

Sit comfortably. Breathe deeply a few times. For 3 minutes, try to remain perfectly still, concentrating on a single thought or idea at the exclusion of all others. Here are some practice ideas on which to practice concentration. You of course can add other ideas to the list, or replace some of these.

For 3 minutes each, concentrate on three or four of the following:

- What you did yesterday
- One thing you learned so far today
- What you enjoy most about a special friend
- Something that is troubling you
- When you laughed last
- Something that recently happened which annoyed you

Now reflect on what you have just done. Were you able to keep focused on the idea? Sometimes it takes some practice to do this, the first time it is difficult with the myriad of thoughts bouncing around in our heads. When you stayed focused, what happened? Did some insights emerge that you previously hadn't considered? Were you surprised by what happened? In what way?

OUR PHYSICAL SELVES

As Dreher (1990) reminds us, "If we neglect our bodies, they become imbalanced and break down" (p. 40). As we often ignore our souls in our rushed lives, we also disregard the physical side of who we are. We take for granted this wonderful biological structure that is also us. One of the most important lessons that many of us learn late is the relation of our bodies to the rest of us. Our emotions, our thoughts, our spirits, and our bodies are all closely tied together.

There are many interesting accounts of illness and mind relationships. A few years ago, Norman Cousins, long-time editor of *The Saturday Review,* became gravely ill. Out of that experience he wrote the book *Anatomy of An Illness* (1979) and later *Head First: The Biology of Hope* (1989). In these books, Cousins illustrates how emotions can combat disease.

Bill Moyers (1993) devoted a TV series and a book to the topic of mind-body relationships. Both Cousins and Moyers go beyond general relationships between body and mind by giving many examples of how the mind actually influences our biology. Cousins (1989) writes, "A biology of emotions is coming into view. For example, discoveries have been made that both the neuroendocrine and immune systems can produce identical substances (peptide hormones, or neuropeptides)" (p. 37).

We need to shift our thinking about our bodies. We must move from thinking about our bodies as mechanical devices that operate like machines, to considering our bodies as biological wonders with soul. As Moore (1992) says, "When we relate to our bodies as having soul, we attend to their beauty, their poetry and their expressiveness. . . . If we could loosen the grip we have on the mechanical view of our bodies. . . . We could exercise the nose, the ear, and the skin, not only the muscles. We might listen to the music of wind in the trees, church bells, distant locomotives, crickets and nature's teeming musical silence. We could train our eyes to look with compassion and appreciation" (pp. 172–173).

EXERCISE 8.3
GETTING IN TOUCH WITH YOUR BODY

Here is a simple exercise for tuning into your body. It can also be used to relax.

Sit in a comfortable chair, but not so comfortable that you may fall asleep.

- Tense the muscles in your toes for the count of ten, then relax. Repeat until you can do it easily.
- Raise your heels until your calves become tense. Lower them and relax.
- Pull in your stomach for the count of ten. Relax.
- Straighten and tense your arms. Relax.
- Bend your elbows and tense your biceps. Relax.
- Tense the muscles across the top of your shoulders. Relax.
- Wrinkle your forehead. Relax.

You may want to write in your journal what you experienced during this exercise.

WRITING

One of the most valuable approaches for learning from the heart is through writing. By systematically writing, we can dig ever deeper into who we are, what we think, how we relate to others, how we relate to nature, and how we connect with the world.

To gain from writing, we must develop a habit of it, we must do it several times a week, better if we are able to do it every day. Julia Cameron (1992) suggests writing three pages every day. She calls this writing the "morning pages. "There is no wrong way to do morning pages," Cameron says. "The morning pages are not supposed to sound smart—although sometimes they might. Most times they won't, and nobody will ever know except you" (p. 10).

Cameron goes on to describe this form of writing as meditation and says, "We meditate to discover our own identity, our place in the scheme of the universe. Through meditation, we find and eventually acknowledge our connection to an inner power source that has the ability to transform our outer world. In other words, meditation gives us not only the light of insight but also the power for expansive change" (p. 14).

For those of us who write as a part of our work, we must take time to write for ourselves, beyond our work. Writing, like so many activities in life, requires constant attention. I've heard often from busy people around me that they plan to do some writing during their vacation or during a holiday break. They find the writing difficult and usually less than satisfying.

It takes time to write in a way that allows us to get in touch with our hearts. Goldberg (1993) says, "... each time we sit down to write we have to be willing to die, to let go and enter something bigger than ourselves. [This kind of writing] includes writing with our whole body, our arms, heart, legs, shoulders and belly. This kind of writing is athletic and alive" (p. 93).

Demons emerge as we write. One of the most pervasive demons in an overpowering censor—that part of ourselves that finds fault with everything that we do. Our censor constantly struggles with our creative self. And too often the censor wins, succeeding in keeping our creative self in the cellar of our lives with the door locked and barred. Occasionally, our creative self slips up the stairs and out the cellar door, but often only for an instant as the censor takes over again. Confronting our censor is a task all of us face. As we write, the censor will say such things as "This writing is awful," and "Don't do this anymore; do something that you know how to do."

As the censor emerges in our writing, confront it. Talk to it in writing. Tell it you respect its perspective, but you want your creative self to have a chance, too. Carry on a written conversation between you and your censor, or between your creative self and your censor self.

Benefits of Writing

Beyond the benefits of regular writing discussed above, there are several others.

Remembering

Through writing, we often can recall details of our past that are hidden away in the deep recesses of our memories.

EXERCISE 8.4   WRITING TO REMEMBER

To effectively do this exercise, you need a timer and something with which to write. It could be a pad and paper, a typewriter, or a word processor. Or, ask a friend to time your writing for you. For each of the following memories, write nonstop for *3 minutes.* Try to focus completely on the question, and do not go back to correct your writing. Keep your censor under control.

• Memory of a sound
• Memory of a tree
• Memory of the color black
• Memory of when you were lonely

When you have completed the exercise, relax. Then go back to read what you have written. Did you turn up any memories that you didn't know you had? What difficulties did you have recalling the memories? What surprises did you experience? Record these insights, and as you record them you may turn up additional ideas.

A challenge many of us face is to stop running from our histories and face them. Writing about our past is one way to stop running.

Reflecting

Stopping to reflect on where we have been, where we are, and where we are headed and the meaning of it all is difficult for many of us. We claim we don't have time for such activity. For some of us reflection is difficult for other reasons. Palmer (1990) says that "Contemplation is difficult for many of us because we have invested so much in illusion. Sometimes we even seem wedded to illusion as a way of survival?" (p. 25).

Examples of illusions Palmer mentions include, ". . . violence solves problems, that both rich and poor deserve their fate. . . ." (p. 25). What illusions get in the way of your reflection? Are you able to keep in check your illusions as you reflect on your life both present and past?

One way to help our reflecting is through the questions we raise. The extent to which we can pose penetrating questions to ourselves and then are willing to attempt answers is the road to authentic reflection. Reflection points us in the direction of our own truth and writing is a powerful way to help it. When we do reflective writing, we are on ". . . a voyage of discovery into the self. Only by going into uncharted territory . . . can a writer find his potential and his voice and his meaning. Meaning, in fact, doesn't exist until [we] go looking for it" (Zinsser, 1988, p. 57).

By reflecting through writing we move toward discovery of deeper meaning in our lives. In our reflections, we often return to life themes that we want to revisit and write more about.

Reclaiming Our Own Truth

We have become a people who depend on other people for our truth. For many of us, the idea of having our own truth is a foreign idea. We claim we don't have enough education, or our position in life is such that we aren't someone to have truth. How unfortunate the pervasiveness of this perspective. Bateson (1994) says we can point at society directly for this state of affairs. "Children learn skills and information in school. . . . They learn notions of authority and truth and limits of creativity. These are the underlying communications of school. For a very large number of children they have been basically negative, a progressive stripping away of dreams, an undermining of confidence" (p. 68).

We all have truth because we have all lived. Our truth is the sense we make of the world, how we have lived, and what we look forward to. The foundation of our truth is our beliefs, values, hopes, fears, joys, and expectations.

Not everyone will agree with our truths. And at times we may not ourselves agree, and we will seek to change them, leaving behind old truths and embracing new ones. But they are our truths. Through writing we can get in touch with them, rediscover them, reclaim them, and applaud them.

Learning from the heart embraces knowing our own truths, for it is in our truth that we can begin to understand one more dimension of who we are. We have two challenges. One is to reclaim our truth for ourselves; the second is to learn to value our own truth and draw on it in a world that generally doesn't value personal truth.

Attending to the Whispers

Amid all of the loud noises in our lives are the whispers. When we write, particularly if we allow ourselves to go deeply into the heart of our writing, we begin to hear the whispers.

Some of the whispers in our lives come from inside of us, the voice that cries, ever so quietly, from our depths. Richard Bode (1993) writes, ". . . I believe we are born with a power to heal our wounds, not through miracles but through a silent voice that speaks to us from within ourselves and won't be stilled, a voice that tells us where to go and what to do, which is a miracle of another kind. It is the refusal to heed that inner voice that causes the incurable sickness of the soul which makes us wither before our time" (p. 100).

Other whispers come from without, the hints of new ideas, the subtle challenges of old ones, the reactions of a friend to what we are saying or doing, the suggestion of something new embedded in something old. To listen for the whispers, we must learn how to make the usual, unusual, to make the ordinary, extraordinary. When we are able to see that which is around us in new ways, the whispers begin.

Through our writing we can hear these whispers and reflect on them.

Where to Write

Some people write in journals daily or several times a week. They use inexpensive notebooks, hardcover books with blank pages, typewriters, or computers. It doesn't matter where or how. I'm still old-fashioned about journal writing. I use a hard cover, blank-page book, and I write with a fountain pen. There is something about the feel of a fountain pen and the flow of ink on a page that makes journal writing different and very special for me. Almost all of my other writing I do on a computer.

Some people I know carry 3 × 5 inch cards, and when they have a spare moment they jot down a thought or question or some new idea they come across. Then, periodically they stick all of their cards in a scrapbook along with other written material, photographs, and clippings. Some simply keep all their 3 × 5 inch cards in a note box, and then riffle through them from time to time—not much different from paging back through the pages of a more formal journal.

Others I know have a 5 × 6" tablet tucked in their purse or brief case. Similar to writing on 3 × 5" cards, these people jot their thoughts on their tablets, tearing out the pages and keeping them in file folders.

It doesn't matter what form you use for writing. What matters is that you write, and write regularly. Writing is clearly a window on our hearts and a powerful approach to learning, yet many of us overlook the opportunity.

CHAPTER 9

Group Approaches

We can enhance learning from the heart by combining individual and group efforts. Learning in a group, without individual struggle, often doesn't go beneath the surface. Individual effort, often penetrating, benefits from interaction, from community. The saying "I cannot be me without you," has much merit.

"Most of life is interdependent, not an independent reality. Most results you want depend on cooperation between you and others," says Steven Covey 1989, (p. 209). Ideas of community and collective thought and action are severely challenged in our society with its extreme emphasis on individualism. We have to work at forming community in this country while ideas of community are pervasive in many parts of the world.

Twenty-four international leaders were asked which values they thought were essential for humans living in the world. They mentioned, love, truthfulness, fairness, freedom, tolerance, respect for life, and responsibility. But they also referred to the need for community, the need for people to learn how to think and act together, not merely live as individuals. (Kidder, 1994). A learning group is one kind of community and can take many forms. Face-to-face classes, workshops, and conferences are familiar to most of us. With technology we can join a learning group even when we are hundreds or thousands of miles from each other. Interactive satellite programs, interactive audio conferencing, and E-mail are examples.

Another kind of learning group occurs when individuals gather to solve some community problem. Their intention for meeting as a group is not first to learn, but to solve a problem or take some collective action. As these groups meet and work on problems, they also learn, and usually profoundly.

Several years ago my wife and I were officers in our local Parent Teachers Organization. At that time, an intersection near our community school was the site of several auto accidents. The intersection became dangerous and it was difficult for youngsters to cross the street. We organized a committee of parents to examine the problem. Representatives from the city traffic department were invited to help us understand possible solutions. They suggested more police enforcement might help to slow the traffic, and they said they would express our concern to the police department.

Some additional enforcement did occur, but the problem persisted. One day, while the parent watched in horror, a child was nearly hit by a speeding auto. The committee began meeting again. The traffic department representative was invited to another meeting, and he assured us that things were getting better and that we should be patient. But we knew things were not getting better.

We sent a formal request for a traffic light to the traffic department. They informed us that traffic was not heavy enough for a light and that we should be patient and the problem would go away. Some of us were patient, for a time, but the problem did not go away.

We continued meeting, this time with our alderman and the chief of police, and demanded a traffic light. We had data on traffic flow through the intersection. We compared our intersection with traffic flow at intersections with traffic lights, and we believed we had a good case. We were turned down again with the excuse that traffic lights were costly and other neighborhoods were ahead of us.

We then organized a community-wide meeting and invited radio, TV, and newspaper reporters, the head of the traffic department, the chief of police, and the mayor. We presented the reasons why we needed a light and asked city representatives to present their perspective. Within a month a new traffic light appeared at our intersection, and the children were safer crossing the street.

We did not call ourselves a learning group, but we certainly were. Each of us learned, and we learned a great deal. We learned how to define and solve a problem and how to work within the system and make the system work. And we learned something about ourselves as individuals and as a group. Never had our Parent Teacher Organization been stronger than at that moment, because we had learned the power and support that can come from group action. We learned from the heart as we learned how to take action.

REASONS FOR LEARNING IN GROUPS

For learning from the heart to occur, a group must be more than a collection of individuals coming together because it is convenient or cost-effective.

For a group to become a group, two-way communication is essential. Often, in a class, workshop or conference, communication is in one direction (from presenter to listener) with little opportunity for participants to interact with each other or with the presenter. To teach from the heart, we must not only be concerned with the subject matter of our work, but also with creating a learning group. Creating a learning group and maintaining it are often more difficult than merely presenting content to a collection of individuals.

Some people, particularly those with little experience or knowledge of benefits, resist efforts to create a learning group. They may tell you that their sole reason for coming is getting what you have to offer, and they don't care about spending time talking to other participants, especially during a class or workshop session. They paid good money to hear you, not each other. Later, after a learning group is formed, many change their minds and discover how rich the experience of a learning group can be.

I also believe that not all people in a group are ready for learning from the heart, including explorations of deeper dimensions of meaning and feeling. For example, participants who are most concerned with advancing on their jobs, finding new jobs, or solving problems they face in their work are often not interested. They want information and new skills, often as quickly as possible, and they don't want to be bothered with whole person learning and the like. Indeed, participants who are not ready for this kind of learning may scoff and make light of people who do want to learn holistically.

As teachers from the heart, we then are faced with a dilemma. Do we abandon any effort to offer opportunities for learning from the heart? That is the easy way out. We can tell ourselves that we are "meeting the needs of the learners," and our obligation is to provide the learning that participants want.

Sometimes, though, when teaching from the heart, we must muster up the courage to meet learners' needs and go beyond those needs. We must provide opportunities for participants to learn from the heart, even though some may initially not be interested and may even resist doing so.

In my experience, particularly in classes and workshops that meet several times over a period of time, almost everyone comes to appreciate such learning. But not all. Sometimes it is years later when I hear from students who tell me that they now understand what I was doing in my class, and that they just weren't ready at that time to deeply involve themselves.

The outcomes of teaching from the heart in groups are several. Groups can provide a mirror for individual learners. They can offer collective support, develop a collective spirit and share a collective truth.

A Mirror

A group of participants can offer each other a mirror. As they try out their ideas and new ways of thinking with each other, these ideas are given a reality check. I encourage participants in my workshops and classes to question each other, not in an unkind, I-can-better-you fashion, but in a caring, loving fashion that allows those being questioned to rethink what they believe and value. Questions are powerful tools for learning—questions from the teacher, but also questions from other participants. To ask a probing question of someone's ideas is a learning experience for both the person asking and the person attempting to answer.

Collective Support

In my workshops where the same group meets several times over the course of a year, and in my graduate classes where we meet weekly for a semester, I organize smaller groups of three to four people within the larger group. I encourage these smaller groups to meet with each other, either by phone, E-mail, or face to face, however they wish to manage it.

These small groups perform a variety of functions. They give each person a chance to share frustrations, lack of understanding, and new ideas and approaches with a small number of people who challenge, question, but above all support and nurture each other.

It is certainly possible for larger learning groups to support and nurture each other as well. And as group members get to know each other, the support function becomes easier. Organizing the smaller groups allows the support function to begin sooner.

A few years ago a young woman in one of my graduate classes, a doctoral student in nutrition science, was planning a career teaching adults. I could see that something was bothering her during the first couple of weeks of the course. She said little during the class discussions and had a tense look about her. She was part of a smaller study group where she had initially shared her concerns. She had told the smaller group that everything we were doing in class flew in the face of what she had observed about teaching. In her experience, she could ask questions of the instructor, but never of another student. And the questioning from this teacher was always of the kind to make the student as uncomfortable as possible. She said the instructor believed that the only way to become a "tough professional" was to learn how to survive in graduate school.

Her small group encouraged her to share her story with the entire group, about 25 of us, at the next class period. Through her tears, she did. It was one of the most powerful moments the class experienced as they identified with the agony this woman faced and then showed their support for her.

Collective Spirit

When a collection of participants becomes a group, a collective spirit often emerges. When asked to describe collective spirit, one group I worked with said this: "It's a sense of oneness," "a feeling of being fully human and alive when I am with these people," "a peak experience," "enthusiasm," "care for each member in the group," "a feeling of joint responsibility for the group—the members together with the instructor," "feeling uplifted," and "being a part of something bigger than oneself." Collective spirit is clearly something more than the sum of the people in the group.

Collective Truth

With many learning groups, a collective truth emerges. As participants struggle with ideas and grapple with relating to each other, a truth that transcends individual efforts begins to emerge. This special truth is usually unique to a particular group. Another group of participants, working on the same topic, will likely develop a different collective truth.

Group members have difficulty expressing the nature of collective truth, just as they have difficulty describing collective spirit. Collective truth includes a realization of the power that rests in a group, particularly when it tackles some problem that no individual could deal with alone. Collective truth includes ideas that emerge from a group as a result of a group's struggle to understand some issue or question. Many would argue that no one individual could have come up with the idea without the presence of the group.

APPROACHES FOR TEACHING GROUPS

A powerful way to learn from the heart is for a group to experience something together, beyond merely listening to someone talk or watching a video.

Drawing

Participants are asked to draw something, tape their drawings on the wall, and then discuss them with the total group.

When I am teaching leadership, I asked participants to draw a picture, using an animal, plant, or bird that depicts them as a leader. The pictures say much about the people and how they view leadership, well beyond the words that they use. For instance, I recently worked with a group where a person drew a picture of a large dog herding a flock of very small sheep. She said she was the dog, and that is how she saw herself as a leader.

Using Three-Dimensional Materials

I often use Legos building blocks in my teaching. I divide a larger group into smaller groups of four or five persons, then give them an assignment. If I am working with a group of teachers of adults, the assignment might be: With Legos, construct how you view learning from the heart. Not only is this a challenge for the group to figure out how to represent something as abstract as learning from the heart with something as concrete as Legos building blocks, but the activity causes a great deal of interaction among the participants. They learn a great deal about themselves in the process, particularly how they relate to other people in a difficult, challenging situation. They often gain some useful and never before considered insights about learning from the heart.

Sharing Stories

J. Murray Elwood (1993) said it well when he wrote, "Storytelling is as natural as breathing, as old as the stone age and as current as Garrison Keillor. People are always sharing stories, whether neighbors in the car pool, business associates over lunch or children at day's end" (p. 10).

In my life-story writing workshops we spend much of our time sharing each other's stories. I ask people to write them first, as a between class activity, and then we share them in class. People learn to know each other at different levels, and soon each person begins to appreciate how much all are gaining from the sharing, both those who share and those who listen.

Story sharing fits many settings. When I am teaching workshops for teachers of adults, I often ask participants to recall a
story when their teaching worked particularly well, recounting
the characters who were involved, the setting, the environment,
and what happened. Recalling one's stories often results in insights that go well beyond the story itself. Often these insights
emerge both in writing the story and in discussing the story when
it is shared with others.

Sharing Journals

In workshops and classes that go on for at least 3 days, I ask
participants to keep a journal. I ask them to write about any
problems or particular challenges they are facing with the course
or workshop, with the interactions that are taking place, with the
pace of the discussions, with how what they are learning relates
to their previous learning, and so on. At the beginning of each
morning session, I take up to an hour asking participants to share
from their journals. I always ask for volunteers and point out that
no one should share anything they are uncomfortable sharing.

These sessions have become powerful tools and provide
wonderful learning opportunities, not only for those who are
sharing, but for everyone else as well. I invite participants to
comment on the journal entries shared, particularly when others
in the group are having similar experiences and thoughts.

As a workshop or class proceeds, and people become more
comfortable and trust each other, journal sharing becomes one
more window on people's hearts.

Listening to Music

In many of my workshops I bring along my tape player and
several music selections. Music is a powerful tool for creating environment, as mentioned above. It also touches people in ways
different from spoken and written words. For instance, I might
have a group listen to Aaron Copland's "Fanfare for the Common Man" and Leonard Bernstein's "America" from *West Side*

Story. Other selections to consider include Vaughn Williams, "To A Lark Ascending" and "Fantasia on Greensleeves"; Sibelius, "Symphony #2 (Allegretto); and Copland's "Appalachian Spring." Almost any music can be used—classical, traditional, jazz, or contemporary.

After listening to the pieces twice, I ask participants to write down the feelings and memories evoked by the presentation, taking time to reflect for a few minutes on what they heard. Finally I ask participants to share what they had written. Usually, there is great diversity in the responses.

Experiencing the Outdoors

Profound learning can occur when we move out of the classroom into the out-of-doors. As described in the prologue, a leadership development group went on a several day canoe trip on the Missouri River, north of Bismarck, North Dakota. Half of the participants had never been in canoes; about that same proportion had not slept in tents before.

As we canoed together down the river, stopping for breaks and meals along the way, a great sense of group camaraderie developed. More experienced canoeists were helping those with less experience. Those with camping experience shared their camping skills with the others.

As we sat around the campfire each evening, with the sparks sifting up through the trees, we shared the stories of the day's experience and what it had meant to us. I encouraged people to write in their journals along the way, and part of the sharing was journal sharing.

After the first day, when people got past their fear of canoeing and their anxiety about sleeping in tents, the learning went ever deeper.

Weeks after the trip was completed and the participants were back home, they continued to share what they had learned during the canoe trip on the river, particularly what they had learned about themselves.

Canoeing and camping are but two of many outdoor activities. Simply sitting outside in a beautiful area and listening to the birds and feeling the warm sun can be a powerful teacher. Likewise, hiking in a wooded area, watching a sunset, quietly gazing at the sky on a moonless night can also accomplish much, particularly for over-stressed, highly busy people who have difficulty slowing down.

EXERCISE 9.1   MYTHICAL JOURNEY

This exercise works best with groups not larger than 20 or 25. Explain that participants are going to experience a mythical journey. They should accept their first thoughts and not think too much about their responses as various directions are given.

The instructions are as follows:

1. Close your eyes and breathe deeply, allowing yourself to relax completely.
2. You are going on a journey. As you begin your journey, you encounter a door. Describe the door. How large is it? Of what is it made?
3. Once through the door, you see a path through a beautiful park-like area. Flowers grow alongside the path, birds are singing in the trees, a gentle breeze caressing you as you walk. How do you feel as you walk along this path?
4. You encounter a wall. Describe the wall. Explain how you move past this wall.
5. Once past the wall, continue along the path. As you walk, you notice that a fog has rolled in and you are not able to see as far or as clearly as you previously did. Out of the mists, and coming on the path toward you is an entity. Describe who or what it is.
6. The entity gives you a message. What is the message?
7. You continue along the path, around an edge of a forest and up a hill. From the top of the hill, you can see a great distance. What do you see?

At this point, I ask people to jot down their answers to each of the situations I have posed. I either hand them a sheet with the words *door, path, wall, entity, message,* and *distant view* written on it, or I project the words on a screen.

After people have had a chance to write down their responses, I ask those who are comfortable to share what they have written. After several minutes of sharing, which usually results in people saying that the process evoked responses that surprised them, I share possible meanings for the various questions.

- The door—gateways and gatekeepers.
- The path—life's journey.
- The wall—barriers we face.
- The entity—our inner goals, our inner self.
- The message—wisdom, criticism, direction.
- The distant view—vision, fears, and hopes for our lives.

I don't use this exercise early in a class or workshop. For many participants, this is an extremely powerful experience, so it is best used after a certain amount of trust has been established and people don't fear sharing with each other.

CHAPTER 10

Challenges

Teaching from the heart doesn't just happen. It takes courage, fortitude, and the willingness to face many challenges. Some of these challenges arise from misperceptions.

PERSONAL CHALLENGES

We all face many personal challenges as we attempt to teach from the heart, which include: other people's opinions, lack of experience, need for personal involvement, and the unpredictable nature of learning.

Other People's Opinions

Many of us grew up with the admonition, What will other people think? whenever we considered doing something different from the norm. I still hear that voice in my head when I am considering trying something that no one else is doing. Trying some of the activities in this book may fall in this category. We immediately assume that when we do something different, people will think less of us. They will criticize us and even poke fun. The easy way is to keep doing what we have been doing. We won't have to worry about what they think, because we already know.

We care what other people think. We don't want to be seen as different or outside what is commonly accepted. Yet, to move ahead, we need to take a risk from time to time. We need to stop being overly concerned with what others will think.

There is also always the surprise that people will consider these new approaches to teaching highly favorably. What they think may be very positive. We won't know until we try.

Lack of Experience

You may not have had much experience teaching from the heart, at least from the perspective that I describe in this book. You come to the task with excitement and dedication, but without the confidence that comes from having done it in a variety of settings. The only way I know to overcome lack of experience is to gain some. Jump into the fray. Work at teaching from the heart, and keep a record of what happens. You may want to record what you try, how it works, how participants react, and the like. Just as a journal can help participants get in touch with their learning, a journal can help you get in touch with what you are learning about teaching from the heart and what you are learning about yourself in the process.

Need for Personal Involvement

Teaching from the heart is not dispassionate, objective, and technical. There are no standard recipes and formulas. As you teach from the heart, you are in touch with *your* heart. It is impossible to help others get in touch with their hearts, if you are not in touch with yours.

Some teachers enjoy objective and technical approaches to teaching. It is comfortable and safe. There is risk when you teach from you heart, because you begin touching the core of who you are. Sometimes you are uncomfortable with what you uncover. The process is no different from what happens with participants. Teaching from the heart is an interaction, a give and take, an involvement of a teacher and learners at a profound level. It also includes role reversal. At times the learners become teachers, and we become learners. For some teachers this is disconcerting. How do you explain that you seem to have lost control—which appears to be happening when learners become teachers?

The key for meeting this challenge is to begin changing our attitudes about teachers and teaching, and recognizing that for learning from the heart to occur, all must be a part of the process, and all must be contributing to it. Control and power are not the issues. Learning is the issue, and what it takes to accomplish it.

The Unpredictable Nature of Learning

Teaching from the heart is fluid, unpredictable, filled with ambiguity, and sometimes even chaotic. Old ideas about linear learning with step-by-step instructions and measurable objectives must be set aside.

"How do I cover the material if I shift gears in midcourse?" is a complaint I hear from teachers. There are certainly times when it is important to cover material, particularly in situations when people must be introduced to certain knowledge and skills in order to accomplish something important or to have background for future learning. Learning CPR, or machine operation, or a highly sophisticated scientific procedure are examples. Usually, though, it is possible to cover the subject matter *and* provide opportunities for learning from the heart. The key is not to become a slave to the material to be covered, and to be open to learning opportunities. It's important to realize that there are many roads to a destination, not merely the one you believed you would follow when you began the course. This is not to suggest that you omit teaching plans with well-developed goals. It does suggest that you must be willing to abandon part of your plan in midjourney, and even, on occasion, change or modify the goal.

CULTURAL CHALLENGES

In addition to the personal challenges, there are cultural challenges to teaching from the heart.

Doing for Its Own Sake

Our society glorifies action and generally disapproves of contemplation and introspection. "We believe in locomotion for its own sake; we think as long as we're flitting from place to place we're going somewhere. We're sprinters running mindlessly against the clock, against ourselves, against the angel of death, and missing the essence of our existence as we go" (Bode, 1993, p. 133).

Teaching from the heart, as well as learning from the heart, requires that we slow down, teachers and learners alike. We become more deliberate. We take time to experience the moment and consider our histories, and we examine our beliefs and values.

At times we may not appear busy, as teachers and as learners. It doesn't look like anything is happening when we watch an egg incubating. Yet, we all know that within the egg, profound change and development are occurring. So it is with learning. To learn from the heart, all of us confront the false god of constant activity and spend some time, without apology, at being ourselves as we learn.

Learning Must Have a Product

The machine age has forced this on us. Why not, we erroneously assume, consider people as machines. We expect a product from a machine, why not expect a product from those who are learning? Why not run our programs for learning as we would run a business, in every way. Palmer (1993) writes, ". . . there are real problems with the image of business community, especially in its tendency to encourage our pragmatic American obsession with 'products' and 'results'. . . . when we get obsessed with results, we take on smaller and smaller tasks, because they are the only ones you can get results with. Ultimately, when we get obsessed with results, we give up educating students and simply train them to pass the test" (p. 5).

When we are teaching from the heart, we are taking on ever larger tasks. It is difficult to think of a larger task than helping people to consider what being human is all about. The product of this effort may not be visible to someone else for sometime, if ever. But does that mean that the learning is not of profound importance?

Someone Else Should Do It

We occasionally hear: learning from the heart doesn't belong in a secular educational program. Keep learning from the heart in the right place, and that right place is in a religious institution.

This line of thinking follows the assumption of segmentation and specialization that is so much a part of our society. If you have a medical problem, consult a doctor; if you have a legal problem, consult an attorney; if you have a spiritual problem, consult a religious leader; if you have a learning problem, consult an educator; if you have an emotional problem, consult a psychologist or psychiatrist; and so on. A specialist for each problem.

Learning from the heart mingles a person's intellectual, emotional, physical, and spiritual dimensions. It at times considers them separately and at other times considers them together. The challenge then is to overcome society's extreme emphasis on specialization, a compartment and specialist for each question and problem, and to realize that we can and must treat people as whole, not as a series of compartments.

INSTITUTIONAL CHALLENGES

If personal challenges, and cultural challenges are not enough, where we teach often provides another set of challenges.

No One Else Teaches This Way

In many teaching settings, you may be the only teacher attempting to teach from the heart. The challenge is to be honest with your fellow teachers, helping them to understand what you are doing, but not judging them if they do not subscribe to your teaching philosophy. Just as there is a right time for many people to accept learning from the heart, there is often a right time for teachers to want to teach from the heart.

Rather than being defensive, invite your fellow teachers to visit your classes and workshops, and see what you are doing, and how participants respond. Invite a fellow teacher who has expressed an interest in such learning to team with you on a session and gain a sense of what it is like to do it. Recently I did this with a colleague who wanted a first-hand experience. Together we taught a semester-long course so he could experience the process directly.

Teaching Is an Intellectual Activity

Throughout society, many people believe that education should mostly ignore emotional, physical, and spiritual activities and concentrate on intellectual activities. Excellence in education usually means intellectual excellence. When we award grades to students, it is based on their intellectual success in a course or class. When teaching awards are given, heavy emphasis is given to the intellectual success of the teacher's students.

Along with an emphasis on intellectualism for teaching and learning come the division of knowledge into disciplines, the development of theories and models, and the adherence to traditional procedures for getting knowledge. Thus teaching, for many, remains within the confines of disciplinary theories, models, and knowledge. With this perspective, there is little room to consider emotional, spiritual, and physical dimensions of learning.

Focusing solely on intellectual development (sometimes with related skill acquisition) is a long standing tradition for many adult education agencies and institutions. When we begin suggesting a broader approach that includes emotional, physical, and spiritual learning, we begin to challenge the status quo.

To face this challenge requires considerable courage and resiliency. Those who have participated in our courses and workshops will come to our aid if there is a chance that what we are doing will no longer be acceptable. Learners are often well ahead of instructors and organizations in their understanding of what learning and teaching can be.

If You Can't Measure It, Don't Do It

Along with products as learning outcomes comes a strong emphasis on measurable outcomes. We've all heard the slogan: You must be able to measure the outcomes of your teaching. It sounds reasonable on the surface, and practical, too. If you can measure the outcomes of something, then it is far easier to show someone what you have accomplished as a teacher and what participants have gained as learners.

Many learning opportunities can and should result in measurable outcomes. But often the most important outcomes are not observable, and may not even be well known to the learner or the teacher. Sometimes the most important learning falls into this category. As we help participants to get in touch with who they are and where they have been, there is no possible way that such learning can or should be measured. But that doesn't mean the learning didn't occur.

I do not mean to imply that we as teachers should avoid being accountable for what we do. Indeed not. But our challenge is to help those to whom we are accountable to understand that some of the most profound learning does not lend itself to measurement. Sometimes the learner's story will help tell what is happening. Other times we can see a difference in how a person relates to people, or carries out a job. Many times, particularly in the short term, there just are no visible outcomes.

For a 3-year leadership development program of which I was a part, I argued with those to whom I was accountable that certain short-term outcomes were available, and some of them could be expressed in measurable terms, but it would take longer for the more important, longer term outcomes to become visible—perhaps as long as 5 years or maybe, realistically, a lifetime. I argued that we too often want immediate results from our educational programs and thus sometimes avoid tackling the more difficult educational challenges. It takes a long time to become a human being. Yet we often want to rush it.

SUMMARY

I discuss these challenges not to frighten anyone away from teaching from the heart, but to remind teachers who want to try it that there are challenges, there are potholes in the road, and the road maps are often not clear. These challenges should not prevent anyone from trying. I can think of nothing more important for a teacher to do than to help people become more human, the ultimate goal of teaching from the heart.

EPILOGUE

The morning following the big storm on the Missouri River, we emerged from our tents, looked around, and began gathering in little huddles to talk about the night, the thunder, and the lightning. Some of the tents had collapsed in the rain and wind and their occupants had gotten wet. Most didn't sleep well. Everyone wanted to talk about the tree near camp that lightning had struck. The blast ripped out shards of wood and scattered them in a circle around the tree's trunk; some stuck in the ground 50 feet away.

The night, and the morning after, provided opportunities for profound connections. Whether or not we wanted to, we had connected to the power and mystery of the natural world. We had felt it, heard it, seen it, and become one with it. The storm had frightened several people. Others transcended their fright and felt the awesomeness of the experience.

In the gray dawn of morning, people wanted to talk, to share their feelings, to exchange stories about how their tent reacted to the storm, to brag a bit, if they were one of the few who came through the storm without at least a wet sleeping bag.

We experienced connections at many levels. We had prepared for the storm as best we could, but we were open to the surprise that comes from learning that has goals but allows for the unexpected, has a teacher, but allows everyone to teach, and allows the setting and the experience to teach as well.

What had we learned about teaching and learning from this experience on the river? For starters, we learned that life itself and the experiences we face can be powerful teachers. We learned that the unexpected, rather than getting in the way of our learning, can become the source for our learning. As teachers, we learned that sometimes the most powerful learning occurs when we get out of the way and let it happen, when we quit trying to control every aspect of what goes on. We try to provide an environment. Then we have faith that people will learn, and what they learn will be good, and will benefit them, and in turn will benefit others.

We all were teachers on the river that cold, damp, drippy morning, when slate gray clouds scudded across the expansive North Dakota sky. We also were all learners.

We experienced learning from the heart firsthand. We lived it. It was so much more than an intellectual experience. We were totally engaged—our intellects, our emotions, our spirits, and our bodies. We felt the joy of wholeness and connections. We experienced the emotions of fear, anger, and the loss of control. All of these are dimensions of teaching and learning from the heart. We had believed we knew exactly what teaching from the heart meant and how to arrange for it. But after this experience, we weren't at all sure what it meant or how to do it. We did emerge with the belief that something special had happened that night on the river, as something special will happen to all of us who work toward teaching and learning from the heart.

REFERENCES

Bach, R. (1977). *Illusions.* New York: Delacorte Press.

Baud, D., & Griffin,V. (1987). *Appreciating adults learning.* London: Kogan Page.

Bateson, M. C. (1994). *Peripheral visions.* New York: Harper Collins.

Bellah, R. N., & Associates. (1985). *Habits of the heart.* New York: Harper & Row.

Bode, R. (1993). *First you have to row a little boat.* New York: Warner.

Bridges, W. (1980). *Transitions.* Reading, MA: Addison-Wesley.

Brookfield, S. (1987). *Developing critical thinkers.* San Francisco: Jossey-Bass.

Cameron, J. (1992). *The artist's way. A spiritual path to higher creativity.* New York: Putnam.

Capra, F. (1983). *The turning point.* New York: Bantam Books.

Chopra, D. (1993). *Ageless body, timeless mind.* New York: Harmony Books.

Cousins, N. (1979). *Anatomy of an illness.* New York: Bantam Books.

Cousins, N. (1989). *Head first: The biology of hope.* New York: Dutton.

Covey, S. R. (1989). *The 7 habits of highly effective people.* New York: Simon & Schuster.

DeAngelis, B. (1994). *Real moments.* New York: Delacorte.

Draves, W. A. (1994). *Energizing the learning environment.* Manhattan, KS: Learning Resources Network.

Dreher, D. (1990). *The Tao of inner peace.* New York: Harper Perennial.

Eiseley, L. (1970). *The invisible pyramid.* New York: Charles Scribner's Sons.

Elwood, J. M. (1993). A search for God in story and time. *America, 169*(11), 10–14.

Estes, C. P. (1992). *Women who run with the wolves.* New York: Ballentine.

Fromm, E. (1956). *The art of loving.* New York: Harper and Row.

Gawain, S. (1978). *Creative visualization.* New York: Bantam.

Goldberg, N. (1986). *Writing down the bones.* Boston: Shambhala.

Goldberg, N. (1993). *Long quiet highway.* New York: Bantam.

Harman, W. (1988). *Global mind change.* Indianapolis: Knowledge Systems, Inc.

Hudson, F. M. (1991). *The adult years: Mastering the art of self-renewal.* San Francisco: Jossey-Bass.

Jones, A. (1985). *Soul making: the desert way of spirituality.* New York: Harper Collins.

Keck, L.R. (1992). *Sacred eyes.* Indianapolis: Knowledge Systems.

Keen, S., & Valley-Fox, A. (1989). *Your mythic journey.* Los Angeles: Tarcher.

Kidder, R. M. (1994). Universal human values: Finding ethical common ground. *The Futurist, 28*(4), 8–13.

Kornfield, J. (1993). *A path with heart.* New York: Bantam Books.

Meizrow, J., & Associates. (1990). *Fostering critical reflection in adulthood.* San Francisco: Jossey-Bass.

Moore, T. (1992). *Care of the soul.* New York: Harper Collins.

Moyers, B. (1993). *Healing and the mind.* New York: Doubleday.

Naylor, T., & Associates. (1994). *The search for meaning.* Nashville: Abingdon.

Palmer, P. J. (1990). *The active life: A spirituality of work, creativity, and caring.* San Francisco: Harper and Row.

Palmer, P. (1993). Remembering the heart of higher education. Address at the American Association for Higher Education Conference, Washington, DC.

Patzer, C. (1924). *Public education in Wisconsin.* Madison, WI: State Superintendent of Public Instruction.

Pearlman, L. J. (1992). *School's out.* New York: Avon.

Peck, M. S. (1987). *The different drum.* New York: Simon and Schuster.

Sark. (1991). *A creative companion.* Berkeley, CA: Celestial Arts.

Storr, A. (1988). *Solitude: A return to the self.* New York: The Free Press.

Stratford, S. (1994, August). Leaders learn to heed the voices within. *Fortune,* pp. 92–100.

Tillich, P. (1948). *The shaking of the foundations.* New York: Charles Scribner's Sons.

Woodward, K. (1994, July). More than ourselves: Havel's declaration of interdependence. *Newsweek,* p. 66.

Zinsser, W. (1988). *Writing to learn.* New York: Harper and Row.

FOR FURTHER READING

Adler, M. J. (1986). *A guidebook to learning.* New York: Macmillan.

Anderson, W. T. (1990). *Reality isn't what it used to be.* San Francisco: Harper & Row.

Apps. J. W. (1979). *Problems in continuing education.* New York: Mc-Graw-Hill.

Apps, J. W. (1985). *Improving practice in continuing education.* San Francisco: Jossey-Bass.

Apps, J. W. (1991). *Mastering the teaching of adults.* Malabar, FL: Krieger.

Apps, J. W. (1994). *Leadership for the emerging age.* San Francisco: Jossey-Bass.

Baldwin, C. (1990). *Life's companion: Journal writing as a spiritual quest.* New York: Bantam.

Baud, D., Keogh, R., & Walker, D. (1985). Promoting reflection in learning: A model. In D. Baud & Associates, *Reflection: Turning exprience into learning,* pp. 18–39. London: Kogan Page, 1985.

Bateson, M. C. (1989). *Composing a life.* New York: Penguin.

Belenky, M. F., Clinchy, B. M., Goldberger, N. R., & Tarule, J. (1986). *Women's ways of knowing.* New York: Basic Books.

Bell, B., Gaventa, J., & Peters, J. (Eds.). (1990). *We make the road by walking: Conversations on education and social change.* Philadelphia: Temple University Press.

Bridges, W. (1991). *Managing transitions.* Reading, MA: Addison-Wesley.

Buber, M. (1958). *I and thou.* New York: Macmillan.

Capra, F. (1975). *The Tao of physics.* New York: Bantam Books.

Castaneda, C. (1993). *The art of dreaming.* New York: Harper Collins.

DePree, M. (1989). *Leadership is an art.* New York: Dell.

Donnelly, D. (1993). *Spiritual fitness.* San Francisco: HarperSanFrancisco.

Ferguson, M. (1980). *The aquarian conspiracy: Personal and social transformation in the 1980s.* Los Angeles: J. P. Tarcher.

Freire, P. (1970). *Pedagogy of the oppressed.* New York: Herder and Herder.

Gilligan, C. (1982). *In a different voice: Psychological theory and women's development.* Cambridge, MA: Harvard University Press.

Giroux, H. A. (1992). *Border crossings: Cultural workers and the politics of education.* New York: Routledge.

Greene, M. (1978). *Landscapes of learning.* New York: Teacher's College Press.

Gross, R. (1991). *Peak learning.* Los Angeles: Tarcher.

Handy, C. (1989). *The age of unreason.* Boston: Harvard Business School.

Handy, C. (1994). *The age of paradox.* Boston: Harvard Business School.

Hanh, T. N. (1991) *Peace is every step.* New York: Bantam.

Harris, M. (1989). *Dance of the spirit: The seven steps of women's spirituality.* New York: Bantam.

Hoff, B. (1982). *The Tao of pooh.* New York: Penguin.

Hoff, B. (1992). *The Te of piglet.* New York: Dutton.

Houston, J. (1987). *The search for the beloved: Journeys in mythology and sacred psychology.* Los Angeles: Tarcher.

Jung, C. G. (1961). *Memories, dreams, reflections.* New York: Vantage.

McLaughlin, C., & Davidson, G. (1994). *Spiritual politics.* New York: Ballentine.

Nerburn, K. (1991). *Native American wisdom.* San Rafael, CA: New World Library.

Nerburn, K. (1993). *The soul of an Indian.* San Rafael, CA: New World Library.

Norris, K. (1993). *Dakota: a spiritual geography.* New York: Ticknor & Fields.

Ornstein, R., & Ehrlich, P. (1989). *New world new mind.* New York: Simon and Schuster.

Palmer, P. J. (1983). *To know as we are known: A spirituality of education.* San Francisco: Harper Collins.

Peck, M. S. (1978). *The road less traveled.* New York: Simon and Schuster.

Peck, M. S. (1993). *A world waiting to be born.* New York: Bantam.

Price, J. R. III, & Simpkinson, C. H. (1993). Sacred stories and our relationship to the divine. In C. Simpkinson & Anne Simpkinson, (Eds.), *Sacred stories: A celebration of the power of story to transform and heal.* San Francisco: HarperSanFrancisco.

Rogers, C. (1977). *On personal power.* New York: Dell.

Vaill, P. B. (1989). *Managing as a performing art.* San Francisco: Jossey-Bass.

Vaughn, R. (1980). *Write to discover youself.* New York: Doubleday.

Wakefield, D. (1990). *The story of your life: writing a spiritual autobiography.* Boston: Beacon Press.

INDEX